CITIZENSHIP
WITHOUT CONSENT

Illegal Aliens
in the
American Polity

PETER H. SCHUCK
and
ROGERS M. SMITH

YALE UNIVERSITY PRESS
New Haven and London

D1068940

Designed by Margaret E. B. Joyner
and set in Zapf International type.
Printed in the United States of America by
Vail-Ballou Press, Binghamton, New York.

Library of Congress Cataloging in Publication Data

Schuck, Peter H.
    Citizenship without consent.

    Bibliography: p.
    Includes index.
    1. Citizenship—United States.   2. Aliens, Illegal—
United States.   I. Smith, Rogers M., 1953-
II. Title
KF4704.S38   1985   323.6'22'0973   85-11968
ISBN 0-300-03530-6 (alk. paper)
ISBN 0-300-03520-9 (pbk. : alk. paper)

The paper in this book meets the guidelines for permanence
and durability of the Committee on Production Guidelines
for Book Longevity of the Council on Library Resources.

10 9 8 7 6 5 4 3 2 1

CONTENTS

ACKNOWLEDGMENTS

The authors wish to acknowledge with gratitude the assistance and support of a number of individuals and organizations. Our fruitful collaboration grew out of a shared intellectual curiosity about the effect of contemporary immigration patterns on American legal and political values and institutions. This curiosity was encouraged, if never fully satisfied, by an occasional interdisciplinary faculty seminar at Yale University on immigration issues, sponsored by the Institution for Social and Policy Studies under the leadership of Richard Nelson. We presented earlier versions of this book to that seminar, as well as to a seminar sponsored by the Program on Migration and Development (part of Harvard's Center for Population Studies), and to a panel of the Association for Public Policy Analysis and Management. We benefited from the comments of participants in those discussions, as well as from those of Professors Bruce Ackerman, Akhil Amar, Perry Dane, Owen Fiss, and Judith Shklar.

While working on this book, Peter Schuck held a John Simon Guggenheim Memorial Fellowship. Rogers Smith's work drew on research completed with the assistance of a

Rockefeller Foundation Fellowship during 1982–83. Research assistance was provided by Suhn Hong, a 1985 graduate of Yale Law School, and was generously supported by Yale Law School. Finally, we wish to express our appreciation to Yale University Press and its senior editor, Marian Neal Ash, for energetically expediting publication.

Peter Schuck dedicates this book to his children, Christopher and Julie, whom he trusts will use their birthright American citizenship to strengthen the great democracy into which they were fortunate enough to have been born. Rogers Smith dedicates this book to Judith Shklar, a citizen by mutual consent and proof that America chooses best when it chooses to be inclusive.

CITIZENSHIP WITHOUT CONSENT

INTRODUCTION

The Americans who fought the Revolutionary War and who ordained the Constitution did not merely transfer their allegiance from one sovereign to another; nor did they simply substitute citizenship in the new nation for subjectship to the British Crown. They were also engaged in a far more radical, imaginative venture—the transformation of the political identity of an entire people. Before the Revolution, the Americans had been the subjects of a royal sovereign, and they inherited their political status as English subjects along with their other patrimonies. By throwing off their allegiance to the Crown, however, they resolved to become something very different—citizens of a new state constituted solely by the aggregation of their individual consents. Voluntary adherence rather than a passive, imputed allegiance was the connective tissue that would bind together the new polity.

This transition to consensually based political membership, however, has never been completed. The original Constitution failed to define the status of citizen or to prescribe how this status could be acquired,[1] although it appeared to contemplate that birth in the United States would confer citizenship automatically, regardless of the choices either of the prospective citizen or of the existing political community. During the antebellum period, courts reinforced this departure from consensual citizenship by refusing to accept any broad right of expatriation that would permit citizens to withdraw from civic membership whenever they wished. But courts also permitted the nation to deny citizenship to native-born Indians and even to free blacks;[2] consensual principles thus perpetuated the oppression of both groups. The upheaval over the status of blacks eventually led, of course, to the adoption of the Fourteenth Amendment and its Citizenship Clause, which provides that "All persons born or naturalized in the United States, and subject to the jurisdiction thereof, are citizens of the United States and of the State wherein they reside."[3] Birthright citizenship thus was formally ratified as the principal constitutive status of the American political community. Since that time, its legitimacy has not been seriously questioned.

Despite the splendor of its constitutional pedigree, however, birthright citizenship is something of a bastard concept in American ideology. For all its appealing simplicity, it remains a puzzling idea. As we shall see, birthright citizenship originated as a distinctively feudal status intimately linked to medieval notions of sovereignty, legal personality, and allegiance. At a conceptual level, then, it was fundamentally opposed to the consensual assumptions that guided the political handiwork of 1776 and 1787. In a polity whose chief organizing principle was and is the liberal, individualistic idea of consent, mere birth within a nation's border seems to be an anomalous, inadequate measure or expression of an individual's consent to its rule and a decidedly crude indicator of the nation's consent to the individual's admission to political membership.

Today the nation is experiencing a new, convulsive violation of consensually based political community: the dramatic increase in the number of undocumented aliens, most of whom are present in contravention of the expressed consent of the political community. The conditions that drive aliens to enter the country illegally often merit sympathy and sometimes even justify the offer of refuge and succor. Nevertheless, the presence of large numbers of illegal aliens in the United States creates significant domestic problems. The aliens themselves are often vulnerable to exploitation because of lack of legal protection; their presence and their possible competition for scarce jobs[4] are sources of ongoing political and ethnic controversy and tension. As the nation's historic experience with slavery indicates, the existence of a large, discrete population that is present within the political community but is ineligible not only for membership but also for many lesser forms of participation in social life cannot fail to provoke continuing political turbulence.

The problem of illegal aliens is compounded, moreover, by a second social transformation—the emergence of the American welfare state. This development has undoubtedly spurred illegal immigration to some extent, but it has also increased the fears and resentments that accompany the presence of illegal aliens. Their need for many social services raises concerns that governmental programs will be seriously overburdened by demands made by people whom the community has designated as outsiders. Regardless of how well- or ill-founded these fears may prove to be (we shall see that the evidence is by no means clear), the history of

ethnic tensions in the United States and elsewhere suggests
that their potential political consequences may be pernicious.
Thus these two social developments, which neither the
Founding Fathers nor the framers of the Citizenship Clause
could have anticipated, raise profound questions about dis-
tributional justice, national autonomy, and political community in contemporary American life. These questions cast
the notions of consensual membership and birthright citizenship in a new and rather different light, dispelling the
obscurity to which their long, unreflective acceptance has
relegated them.

To explore these issues, this book will elaborate an important but previously neglected dichotomy between two
radically different conceptions of political community, which
we call the "ascriptive" and the "consensual." In its purest
form, the principle of *ascription* holds that one's political
membership is entirely and irrevocably determined by some
objective circumstance—in this case, birth within a particular sovereign's allegiance or jurisdiction. According to this
conception, human preferences do not affect political membership; only the natural, immutable circumstances of one's
birth are considered relevant.

The principle of *consent* advances radically different
premises. It holds that political membership can result only
from free individual choices. In the consensualist view, the
circumstances of one's origins may of course influence one's
preferences for political affiliation, but they need not do so
and in any event are not determinative.

In light of these contrasts, this book will propose and
defend an essentially consensual ideal of citizenship. Such
a citizenship, we shall argue, would be more legitimate in

theory, more flexible in meeting practical policy problems, and more likely to generate a genuine sense of community among all citizens than the existing scheme, while protecting the established human rights of aliens. To those ends, we shall advocate a combination of measures to render American citizenship law more consensual than it has previously been and to ameliorate what is the greatest contemporary threat to a consensually based political community—the massive presence of illegal aliens. We shall propose four related reforms: first, more effective enforcement of existing immigration laws; second, a system of realistic, credible employer sanctions to remove the chief incentive to most illegal immigration; third, more generous legal admission policies, especially within this hemisphere; and fourth, a reinterpretation of the Fourteenth Amendment's Citizenship Clause to make birthright citizenship for the children of illegal and temporary visitor aliens a matter of congressional choice rather than of constitutional prescription.

The first three of these proposals are extensively discussed in the existing policy literature, so other than noting their importance, we shall not pursue them at length here. The proposal relating to birthright citizenship, however, has to our knowledge never been seriously considered.[5] We speculate that this unquestioning acceptance has persisted for many reasons—perhaps because the Fourteenth Amendment has been thought to render our position unconstitutional, perhaps because the problem of illegal aliens has only recently reached critical proportions, or perhaps because the status quo has achieved the tyranny of the familiar. In any event, we shall argue that the phrase "subject to the jurisdiction thereof" in the Citizenship Clause (what we call the "jurisdiction requirement") expresses a constitutional commitment to citizenship based on mutual consent—the consent of the national community as well as that of the putative individual member. If we are correct, our interpretation of birthright citizenship is both constitutionally permissible and democratically legitimate. We shall also argue that, quite apart from the problem of the membership status of illegal aliens and their offspring, a more consensual citizenship also requires that Congress take two further steps. It should establish a more practical procedure for voluntary expatriation, and it should adopt naturalization policies that are more inclusive of those born overseas to American citizen parents.

The book consists of five chapters. In chapter 1, we develop the ascriptive and consensual conceptions by identifying their main sources in English political theory, isolating their characteristic assumptions and elements and analyzing the formal legal rules of citizenship to which their distinctive logics lead. We argue there that, while both conceptions have certain advantages, the consensual position possesses far more moral weight today and should be strengthened as much as is consistent with the recognized human rights of aliens. In chapters 2 and 3, we trace how, despite America's commitment to consent, its law of citizenship nevertheless came to be based primarily on birthright citizenship, an essentially ascriptive status. By examining the pre–Fourteenth Amendment law of United States citizenship and the amendment's Citizenship Clause, we illustrate how ascriptive and consensual conceptions have always competed for dominance in American law and how the Fourteenth Amendment, even as it constitutionalized a form of ascriptive citizenship, moved significantly toward the consensual view. In chapter 4, we review the two major social transformations—the growth of illegal migration and an enlarged welfare state—which are affecting and being affected by the role of birthright citizenship today and which necessitate its reappraisal. In chapter 5, we conclude that the United States should, both as a matter of principle and of policy, continue its historical movement toward a more consensually based citizenship, albeit one that continues to protect those legitimate human interests which birthright citizenship does in fact advance. We therefore propose the changes in citizenship law described above and defend our proposal against a number of anticipated objections.

These proposed changes, we believe, are important, and several will be highly controversial. They would mean that the native-born children of undocumented aliens and of nonimmigrant (that is, temporarily visiting) aliens would become citizens at birth only if Congress so decided. Responsibility for defining the boundaries of the political community would rest, as we believe it should, with the representative organs of the nation. Second, American citizens who wished to expatriate themselves would be able to exercise their right to renounce citizenship more knowledgeably, meaningfully, and readily. Finally, naturalization policies would be more inclusive of children born to American citizens overseas. More generally, we urge that the festering problem of illegal immigration should be combatted, and the national commitment to a liberal consensualism vindicated, not just by restrictive measures such as stricter enforcement, employer sanctions, and denial of birthright citizenship to children of illegal and nonimmigrant aliens. Although these policies are meritorious, they are insufficient, and must be coupled with more generous admission and naturalization policies.

1 TWO CONCEPTIONS OF CITIZENSHIP

The customary division of national laws of citizenship into the "principles" of *jus soli* (place of birth) or *jus sanguinis* (line of descent) denotes the objective criteria most often used to determine one's citizenship. But the conceptions of political membership that have vied for supremacy in Anglo-American law implicate a different, more fundamental dichotomy—one between the rival principles of ascription and consent.[1] These principles reflect quite distinct understandings of the origins, nature, and obligations of political communities, and each promotes certain values that Anglo-American legislators and judges have embraced at different times and often simultaneously. Each, however, also involves certain difficulties that these decision-makers have tried to avoid. Neither principle, then, seems wholly satisfactory in its pure form. At least since the eighteenth century, therefore, Anglo-American law has embodied compromise doctrines that combine certain features drawn from each conception in the hope of producing pragmatic satisfaction, if not theoretical coherence. As we shall see, however, the two principles are not so easily blended.

The principle of ascription was present in much medieval

thought, but its implications are best exemplified by Sir Edward Coke and Sir Robert Filmer. Both men wrote at a time when European monarchies generally, and the English Crown in particular, were still striving to unite fragmented territories and create centralized national governments to replace a feudal order that divided power among diverse regional lords and religious authorities. The English monarchs confronted the special tasks of cementing their rule over Scotland and Ireland in Coke's day and of resisting Calvinist revolutionaries and Whig reformers in Filmer's. Consequently, these authors mobilized arguments for a strong duty of obedience to the royal sovereign. Among these arguments was the ascriptive view of political membership, which imposed perpetual allegiance on the subject.

The principle of consent also has ancient and medieval antecedents, but the first writers to present it in something like its modern form were the Puritan revolutionaries and the political theorists of the late-seventeenth- and eighteenth-century Enlightenment, best represented by John Locke. The Puritan thinkers wished to discredit claims for a divinely ordained hierarchy in human society that supported priestly as well as secular authority.[2] The Enlightenment writers shared this concern, but they wished to challenge more broadly all of the social institutions of the medieval Christian order—indeed, its entire underlying world view. That order, they believed, shackled intellectual progress and spiritual liberty by perpetuating superstition; stifled economic progress by maintaining outmoded restrictions and aristocratic privileges; and denied political freedom by legitimating autocracy. They hoped to revitalize their world by placing political society on a new, explicitly consensual footing, which would erode the authority of the feudal elites and infuse all social institutions with a responsiveness to current ideas and needs and to what they took to be the natural rights of mankind. This aim led Locke, in particular, to reject birthright citizenship for the very reason that Coke and Filmer had endorsed it—because it served to ascribe a political membership and allegiance to those who never freely chose them.

But the idea of consent, like the idea of equality, is not easily cabined; by the late eighteenth century, radical Enlightenment theorists such as William Godwin found even the social contract too restrictive. To Godwin, government by consent pointed logically to rational anarchism, a position he energetically embraced and defended. Coke, Filmer, Locke, and Godwin therefore enable us to trace the implications of the ascriptive and consent principles. The oppressiveness of Coke and Filmer's defense of perpetual allegiance to an absolute sovereign, Locke's potential for discriminatory exclusion, and Godwin's anarchic tendencies also suggest why Anglo-American law has been reluctant to embrace either principle in an undiluted form.

In the remainder of chapter 1, we shall use these writers to explore the implications of these principles along four conceptual dimensions. First, we consider the source and justification of political membership. Second, we consider the nature and duration of the obligations that membership entails. Third, we consider the relationship between the obligations of political membership and those that arise out of other memberships, particularly those of the family. Finally, we examine the advantages and disadvantages of the ascriptive and consensual views.

The Principle of Ascription

English law assumed from antiquity that all persons born within the dominions of the Crown, whether of English or alien parents, were English subjects. Writing from the vantage point of the 1860s, Sir Alexander Cockburn argued that this birthright rule was natural enough when England was an insular island society with few aliens present and few English subjects abroad.[3] But English law did not expressly refer to the principle of *jus soli*, while royal decrees and statutes formally established by the mid-fourteenth century that neither members of the royal family nor the children of English subjects could lose any rights due to birth outside the king's domains.[4] No theory of membership that could account for these diverse precedents was formally elaborated until 1608, when Sir Edward Coke reported the decision reached by himself and fourteen other judges in the landmark *Case of the Postnati*, better known as *Calvin's Case*.[5]

The case arose in a context conducive to extreme assertions of royal power, for it presented the leading members of the English bench with the question of the extent to which the accession to the throne of England of James I, already James VI of Scotland, had unified the two states. The central legal issue concerned whether Robert Calvin, a child born in Scotland in 1606 after James's accession, could inherit lands in England as a native or whether he was an alien and therefore ineligible to inherit under English law. While Coke opposed unlimited royal power, he nonetheless thought it vital to assert that the political union created by the accession overrode all preexisting national allegiances.[6]

To support this conclusion, he elaborated "the first comprehensive theory of English subjectship."[7] His theory based
that status so firmly on the ascriptive principle that later
advocates of membership by ascription, such as Filmer, only
extended elements of Coke's basic framework. Indeed, Coke's
position remained the universally cited starting point for
Anglo-American legal analyses of political membership
through at least the nineteenth century.[8] By articulating this
conception, Coke was able to establish once and for all the
common membership of Scottish and English *postnati* in
one united community of allegiance, regardless of any contrary indications in any past or future man-made law—
English, Scottish, Roman, common, or statute. To reach this
result, Coke appealed to natural law to "direct this case,"
thereby giving birthright political membership the strongest
possible sanction.[9]

Source of Membership

Coke's entire analysis rested on the ascriptive view that
one's political identity is automatically assigned by the circumstances of one's birth. Coke understood political identity
as being at root a question of one's allegiance as a subject
to some sovereign. At birth, every person acquired such an
allegiance.[10] This relationship of allegiance was fundamental and inescapable.[11] Coke stressed, moreover, that birth
within a particular allegiance did not truly depend on the
geographic location or physical circumstances of one's na-
tivity.[12] One could be born within the king's allegiance even
if not born within his dominions. One could also be born
within the king's dominions "without obedience" and thus

not be "a natural subject."[13] For Coke, then, it was the community of those with a common allegiance, not communities of common languages, ethnic origins, or geographical location, that determined one's political membership.[14]

If not place of birth, what led to the ascription of an individual's subjectship to some sovereign? On this point Coke was not altogether clear. Appealing to "birth within the allegiance" was obviously circular. The decisive element appears to have been birth under circumstances in which the sovereign possessed the power to provide protection to the subject and was actually exercising it to at least some minimal degree.[15] This understanding also accounted for the established exceptions to the general rule of *jus soli*. If the English wives of the king's ambassadors had children in a foreign land, the latter were nevertheless "natural born subjects," for they were still under the power and protection of their monarch. But if alien enemies should occupy English soil and have children there, "that issue is no Subject to the King," for they were not born under his power or protection.[16] Children born to English subjects residing in other lands raised a more complex question. They could be said to be still under the power and protection of the English Crown, since their parents owed allegiance to it and were normally entitled to some protection from it. On the other hand, the children were clearly under the direct power of another sovereign, benefiting from the civil peace that this other, more proximate sovereign had established.

Coke did not address this issue directly, but he readily conceded that for all who were born in a land to which their parents were aliens, "there must of necessity be several kings, and several ligeances."[17] All individuals' obligations were determined by the extent of protection that they had received at birth, not by their parents' allegiance per se. The alien parent owed only temporary "local obedience" to the sovereign in whose land he resided, but that was "strong enough to make a natural subject" of his child.[18] Yet although Coke treated the allegiance to the sovereign who had most direct power over the infant at birth as most natural and therefore primary, the child could also have obligations to the sovereign of his parents and could acquire obligations to additional sovereigns later in life. Each of these relationships imposed valid and binding allegiances, however much they might conflict with one another.[19] As to why birth within a sovereign's power and protection should generate the most fundamental political tie, birthright subjectship with allegiance to that sovereign, Coke gave a distinctively ascriptive answer: "Ligeance or Obedience of the Subject to the Sovereign is due by the Law of Nature."[20] Because this relationship followed the law of nature, it was impervious to human choice.

Coke treated the relationship of subject to sovereign as natural in two distinct senses. Each drew on then prevalent conceptions of how political life was embedded in the natural world. First, this relationship was natural because it stemmed from a seemingly "natural" debt that each infant owed to his lord, a debt of allegiance due in return for protection received. Because the sovereign's power assured some measure of peace and safety for the child at birth, a time when the infant was wholly vulnerable, the child was permanently obligated to him. Today it would seem peculiar to speak of an infant as indebted for a protection he never sought and of which he was quite unaware, and we may think it implausible to attribute to the sovereign a concern to provide such security. But the belief that a natural obligation existed under these circumstances reflected a widely accepted cosmology. To men like Coke, the universe consisted of divinely created hierarchical relationships between superiors and inferiors, in which each person was assigned an appropriate role within the "great chain of being."[21] In this view, each person was inevitably born under, and was bound to obey, the dominion of some superior who in turn owed reciprocal duties to his subject inferiors. This hierarchy and its correlative obligational system were sanctioned by God, who placed each person in his permanent position.[22]

The second way in which the sovereign's authority over subjects was thought to be natural was by analogy to the father's natural authority over his children.[23] Filmer was the leading expositor of this rather strained analogy, arguing that legitimate kings had historically been either the "natural parents" of their peoples, or "the next heirs to those first progenitors" who held that status. In that way, they could "in their right succeed to the exercise of supreme (paternal) jurisdiction."[24] Although Coke in *Calvin's Case* did not explicitly employ the analogy, his reasoning seemed to depend upon it.[25]

Again, while this paternal analogy seems dubious today, it strongly appealed to those who saw the natural order reflected in political society. We stress the pervasiveness of this patriarchal view because it explains why many subsequent critics of political authority, like Locke, felt compelled to advance new views of the family.[26] It also explains why, as discussed below, changing conceptions of family roles almost automatically altered the nature of debate about political membership.

Nature and Duration of Obligations of Membership

These views concerning the "natural" source and justification for birthright membership in a community of allegiance defined the obligations that were ascribed to both subject and sovereign. In brief, the subject owed complete obedience and service; the sovereign owed physical protection and just governance. Being imposed by the eternal law of nature, which was prior to all man-made laws, both obligations were perpetual and immutable; to Coke, they were obligatory in all times and places and not "confined only to England." Even if the sovereign became unable to protect his subject, the subject's obligation remained, now augmented by an obligation to whatever other sovereign had power over him.[27] Similarly, the law of nature always required a sovereign to provide at least minimal protection to all his subjects; even Parliament could not relieve the king of this obligation.[28]

But the king's failure to provide this minimal protection would not alter the allegiance that the natural-born subject owed him for the protection afforded during the subject's infancy. Consequently, no right to disobey or to expatriate oneself could arise. Indeed, expatriation and denationalization—termination of the allegiance between a natural-born subject and his sovereign by either the individual or the government—were considered contrary to natural law and therefore impossible for either party. A

birthright subject was perpetually bound to his birthright
sovereign regardless of his parentage, his own desires, or
even those of his king. Other allegiances could be added,
but one's membership in a sovereign's community of allegiance was irrevocable.[29]

Employing the analogy between royal and paternal authority, Filmer reached identical conclusions about the nature and duration of the obligations between sovereigns and
subjects. The king, divinely charged with the "universal fatherly care of his people," was bound to "preserve, feed,
clothe, instruct, and defend the whole commonwealth." But
these sweeping obligations, which stemmed from the "law
of nature," created no rights of disobedience should the
sovereign falter, even as to royal violations of divine law.
The king was "supreme," with "unlimited" jurisdiction to
govern "by no other law than by his own will." Filmer
grounded this view on a defense of unlimited parental authority, to which the king had allegedly succeeded. He argued that the father had absolute "dominion of life and
death" over his children, and that the law of nature sub-
ordinated children to this power forever.[30]

For Filmer, then, as for Coke, the natural status of subjectship imposed mutual but asymmetrical obligations:
subjects had to obey, sovereigns should protect, but sovereign authority was unlimited so far as the subjects were
concerned. The obligations of allegiance remained even if
the sovereign did not protect, for only God could limit his
appointed rulers. Each party's obligations, moreover, were
perpetual in just the way that a son and his natural father
could never shed their natural obligations to one another.

Political Membership and Rival Allegiances

The paternal analogy became problematic, however, by creating a potential conflict between the absolute power of a subject's natural father and that of his sovereign. This potential conflict was similar to that existing between one's allegiance to the local lord and to the king; as such, it raised the larger question of the relationship between the obligation of allegiance to one's sovereign and obligations growing out of other ascribed statuses. Most advocates of the ascriptive view wanted to affirm that allegiance to the royal sovereign was the highest allegiance of man over man. It was established by God in his hierarchical ordering of the universe and could be overridden only by God. But since Filmer had held that the king succeeded to the antecedent power of natural fathers over their children, the possibility that family obligations might rival political ones caused him great difficulty. Most proponents of royal absolutism feared a return to feudalism's earlier stages, in which kinship-based local allegiances had competed with claims of royal prerogatives.[31] Having relied so heavily on the paternal analogy, Filmer wished to retain the authority of kinship claims while still upholding centralized rule.

His response was simply to assert, without argument, that parental authority was "subordinate and inferior" to that of the monarch, who was the "father over many families"; he held the rank of the original and therefore supreme patriarch of the extended family that was his commonwealth.[32] This argument, of course, rested upon Filmer's claim that the monarch had somehow inherited or been assigned full and natural parental authority over his people. Coke similarly affirmed the legitimacy of natural paternal authority while treating the father as subordinate to the king.[33]

Advantages and Disadvantages

The ascriptive views of Coke and Filmer, although deployed by them for particular political purposes, nonetheless possess more universal attractions. The paternal analogy does capture a widely shared moral intuition: many persons feel indebted to those who have nurtured them, including the broader political community into which they were born, despite the fact that they did not initially choose to receive that aid. Because our community shapes our identity, our sense of who we are, it may indeed seem natural to feel that one belongs in one's country and owes it allegiance in a way that can never be entirely extinguished. Many also feel that the nation should take responsibility for all those who, through no fault of their own, depend upon it in their most vulnerable years. Indifference to the needs of infants is obviously cruel, and the ascriptive view promises protection to all those thus situated. On a more mundane level, ascription appears to provide clear, simple rules that avoid many complicated questions of nationality and allegiance. As a practical matter, place of birth ordinarily suffices to indicate whether an allegiance can be said to exist.

But for all this, the ascriptive view entails several serious problems. First, it significantly constrains individual freedom, however one defines that concept. Birth binds one irrevocably to a particular community of allegiance. According to most modern notions of political freedom, it seems morally wrong to ascribe to an infant inescapable obligations that may, for example, eventually require him to violate his conscience or even jeopardize his life by participating in a war he thinks unjust. Second, ascription significantly constrains governmental control over membership and can even compel the state to provide protection to those, most notably illegal aliens, whose entrance to the country it has actively endeavored to prevent.[34] Finally, the formulations of the ascriptive principle provided by Coke and Filmer create multiple allegiances. Filmer by implication, and Coke explicitly, permit weaker, more consensual, but still valid allegiances to coexist with the fundamental obligation to the sovereign who provided protection in one's infancy.[35] When conflicts arise, the ascriptive view cannot resolve them. In *Calvin's Case*, for example, a sovereign wished to assert the primacy of natural subjectship, but in other circumstances he would have favored a different priority, emphasizing instead his claims to the overriding allegiance of children born of his subjects abroad, of naturalized subjects, or of resident aliens. Today, this problem persists in the ambiguous and inconsistent relationships created by dual citizenship.

Because of these problems and others, the seventeenth century, which began with Coke's endorsement of birthright subjectship in *Calvin's Case*, saw sweeping challenges in both England and America to the world view that the ascriptive principle reflected. New, linked conceptions of cosmos, polity, and family undermined beliefs in an all-encompassing natural hierarchy governing all three realms: in the great chain of being, in the divine right and unlimited authority of kings, and in equally unlimited and perpetual paternal authority over the family. These changes inevitably rendered problematic the legal doctrine of birthright subjectship. If questions of political membership have been settled by appeal to natural law, as they were by Coke, what were courts to do when conceptions of the content, even the existence, of natural law altered? A tempting answer was to embrace membership based on consent alone. But that ideal, too, presented fundamental and inescapable difficulties.

The Principle of Consent

The assaults on the medieval world of Coke and Filmer that produced political and ideological revolutions in England and America challenged not only governmental absolutism but also patriarchal supremacy. That dual focus was necessary because, as we have seen, paternal and political rule were both defended as ordained by nature, and apologists for autocracy often relied on the more obviously natural authority of fathers to buttress monarchical claims, especially the claim to the perpetual birthright allegiance of native-born subjects. Consequently, when Enlightenment proponents of limited, consensual government sought to challenge absolutist views, they had to reconsider the "natural" authority of fathers over children, its implications for state power, and thus how the circumstances of birth defined one's political membership.

This reconsideration appeared most clearly in the works of John Locke. For example, in each of his *Two Treatises of*

Government, Locke took as his main opponents those defenders of the old order who argued that "Everyone is born a Subject to his Father, or his Prince, and is therefore under the perpetual tye of Subjection and Allegiance."[36] The historian James Kettner views Locke as the theorist who best exemplified the transition from ascriptive subjectship to consensual citizenship. Despite some recent reservations about the influence of Locke's *Second Treatise* in America, the choice is appropriate.[37] Nonetheless, as we shall see, Locke failed to address many important issues raised by consensual government. These issues are more central to the different intellectual tradition of consensual political community that historian J. G. A. Pocock refers to as "civic humanism" or "republicanism."[38] Because these republican ideas also influenced the American conception of consensual citizenship, we shall note their pertinent features as we develop the predominant, Lockean understanding of consent as the constitutive principle of political community.

Source of Membership

Locke's familiar doctrine of government by consent, with its attendant right of revolution, was based on his radically new view of the relationship of children to their parents and to the polity, a view that stemmed in turn from a thoroughgoing rejection of the medieval portrait of society as a natural, organic hierarchy. To Locke, the most fundamental fact about children was that they were creatures of God, intended to occupy that equal and independent status that is the natural condition of mature, rational beings. This fact, for Locke, defined the limited nature of parental

and political authority. Locke agreed that the family was a
natural social unit and that parents properly possessed some
dominion over their offspring during minority. He maintained, however, that this authority rightfully belonged to
both parents, not simply to the patriarchal father.[39] And he
insisted, even more vehemently, that parents possessed only
limited, tutelary authority over their children, and possessed
this authority only while the latter remained incapable of
rational self-governance. He described this authority as a
natural duty to support and educate the children so that
they could become competent, independent adults. That
duty could never justify absolute power over the child's life
or over property derived by the child from a nonparental
source. Upon reaching maturity, moreover, the child owed
only honor and esteem, not obedience, to his parents, and
should thereafter relate to them as friends and equals.[40]

This view obviously precluded use of the paternal analogy
to defend absolute political sovereignty. But Locke went
further, arguing that only the parents had any measure of
natural rule over a child. He denied that political membership and allegiance were natural in any sense: far from
acquiring a civic identity at birth, a child could not truly
become a subject of any political ruler until adulthood. Political allegiance could originate only from an act of personal
consent, which only adults were competent to perform.

The state did possess a limited jurisdiction over children,
for its duties stemmed not only from the consensual will of
its citizens; it also had to conform to the obligations imposed
by the natural human rights that Locke held to be the in-
violable and inalienable endowment of all persons. As an
authorized executor of the law of nature, the state thus had

to protect the child's rights to life, property, and education should the parents arbitrarily violate their duties to the child.[41] Yet natural law empowered the state to restrain violations of *anyone*'s human rights, including resident aliens.[42] Locke repeatedly insisted that the child was otherwise subject only to the limited natural authority of his parents.[43] A child, then, could not be a government's subject because subjectship must be based on the tacit or explicit consent of an individual who had reached the age of rational discretion.

Locke noted that the child could only inherit the father's property in accordance with the laws of the parent's political society, which usually required the legatee to be a subject. At the age of majority, therefore, children usually *chose* (at least tacitly) to be members of their father's polity, a pattern that accounted for the widespread "mistake" of thinking that children were naturally subject to it. Instead, Locke insisted: "*a Child is born a subject of no Country and Government*. He is under his Father's Tuition and Authority, till he come to Age of Discretion; and then he is a Free-man, at liberty what Government he will put himself under; what body politick he will unite himself to."[44] Locke even believed that this view was implicitly admitted in practice, for he asked rhetorically, "who ever was judged as a *Traytor* or *Deserter*, if he left or warr'd against a Country, for being barely born in it of Parents who were Aliens there?"[45] One answer, of course, is that Coke had so judged. But it was inconceivable to Locke that the accident of birth in a land foreign to one's parents should create permanent obligations to that country. Undoubtedly, he would have been astonished that children of illegal aliens might acquire membership in a country by birth. Even in the case of children of members, not to speak of children of legal or illegal aliens, ascriptive obligations were explicitly and emphatically rejected in favor of a thoroughgoing consensualism.

While Locke argued that civic membership should rest on consent, however, he recognized that other factors largely determined one's national and political identity in actuality, either by influencing personal choice or, most commonly, through legal ascription of citizenship. Although he opposed such ascription, Locke assumed, without much discussion, that people would in fact choose to live in political communities with those to whom they had affective ties, usually due to familial, tribal, linguistic, religious, or ethnic kinship. His notion of consensual citizenship thus presupposed that choices of political membership would conform to "natural ties of the sort that modern conceptions of the nation" associate with national identity.[46] But he did not stress this expectation because he wished to deny what medieval thought had maintained—that such particular ties irrevocably mandated one's status. Should individuals decide to join new communities, abandoning previous personal affiliations, and should those communities accept them, these choices must be recognized as equally legitimate.

Given his political and philosophical purposes, Locke's radically consensualist position was understandable. But his aims also led him to neglect some difficult questions about purely consensual political membership that are highly relevant in the American context. Perhaps most important, a genuine sense of common civic identity may not be sustainable if consensual citizenship should lead to an excessive diversity of languages, ethnic origins, social customs, economic statuses, and religious beliefs within one political society. On this issue, among others, American thought was influenced not so much by Locke's individualistic liberalism as by an alternative tradition of discourse on consensually based citizenship, the tradition Pocock has labeled "Atlantic Republicanism."[47]

That republican tradition, carried on by writers such as James Harrington, Montesquieu, and Jean-Jacques Rousseau, is usually portrayed as advancing an ideal of active, public-spirited citizenship in contrast to the Lockean view of civic membership, which simply guarantees protection for private pursuits. There is, moreover, a lively debate concerning how far either "republicanism" or "liberalism" thus understood can be said to have dominated the nation's political consciousness at various periods.[48] But this debate need not occupy us here, for however disparate their senses of what civic life should demand, writers in these two traditions did not differ greatly in regard to the consensual basis of citizenship. Rousseau as much as Locke stressed that society must be seen as originating in a social contract, with membership stemming from the free mutual choice of existing and prospective citizens.[49]

But unlike Locke, republican thinkers such as Montesquieu and Rousseau did reflect extensively on the sorts of social characteristics that would make it possible to sustain a society predicated on consent and to inspire the strong patriotism and ethos of civic service that republicanism esteemed. Their analyses insisted that if republics were to foster a powerful sense of civic identity and devotion, they must be small and homogeneous, with citizens socialized to be "like a single family."[50] Hence they favored a variety of internal measures to promote unity of belief and conduct, including censors, enforcement of a common civil religion, numerous public rituals, ceremonies, holidays, and restraints on economic diversity.[51]

These concerns led republican thinkers to acknowledge an implication of the consent principle that remained muted in Locke: consent must be mutual, and members of an existing community could properly refuse consent to the membership of those who would disrupt their necessary homogeneity. Virtually all republican writers stressed the importance of keeping the republic small, which could only be accomplished if immigration were sharply limited. Aristotle, whom Pocock sees as the progenitor of republican thought, argued that aliens should be admitted to citizenship only if there were a great dearth of citizens; ordinarily, citizenship should be confined "to those who are of citizen parentage on both sides."[52] Rousseau agreed that foreign perspectives must be limited within the community, particularly in regard to education of the young.[53]

Here, republican thought generated a fundamental internal tension, for while it may be destructive of a republic's unity and homogeneity to enlarge its domain, the republic may risk direct conquest and destruction if it remains small. Republican theorists pondered at length whether a republic could safely expand through a policy of imperialism involving the conquest and absorption of diverse lands and peoples. Some, like Montesquieu and Rousseau, argued against such policies, insisting that it would be harmful to the republic to include within it large numbers of persons who were barred from the political participation that was the core of republican citizenship. Hence conquests should not add more citizens than could be included within the demos of a small republic.[54] Others, like Machiavelli, argued that only an imperial policy was safe, and that republics must rule conquered rivals as subject peoples, not as fellow citizens.[55] As Pocock notes, however, both camps agreed that a republic was not bound "to accord the rights of humanity" to "noncitizens."[56]

Correspondingly, those actual republics which did not actively engage in imperialism, such as Sparta, usually relied heavily on the labor of a large slave population that obviously participated in many ways in the life of the community but was denied citizenship. Aristotle (as well as many republicans of the American Revolutionary era) viewed this practice as essential.[57] The ancient republics also made it very difficult for outsiders to obtain citizenship; Athens, for example, left large numbers of persons, including Aristotle himself, as permanent resident aliens or "metics." There was little question, then, that new citizens had to obtain the consent of the political community as well as exercise their own volition to join, and that a republic could and ordinarily would exclude from citizenship even large numbers living permanently within its bounds, as well as nonresident aliens.[58] As discussed below, when the United States was founded, these republican arguments about the necessity to preserve communal homogeneity and processes of character formation conducive to free institutions were central to early discussions of immigration and naturalization policies. In keeping with the republican tradition, the community's power to refuse consent to the membership of those who would disrupt their necessary homogeneity was never seriously questioned.

Locke's failure to discuss the issues of whether the community may refuse consent to new members or denationalize existing ones may simply have reflected his belief that since governments were normally eager to admit and keep citizens, it was the individual's power to withhold consent, not the community's, that needed emphasizing. His omission accorded, too, with his more liberal stress on natural individual rights, personal choice, and freedom for private pursuits, in contrast to the focus on the common good and political participation that dominated republican discourse. Here we encounter a recurring, fundamental tension in liberal thought: liberals like Locke wished to base governmental legitimacy on consent, yet they also wished to insist that there were minimal but fundamental human rights that could never be legitimately violated, even if all concerned parties consented.[59]

Locke characteristically dealt with this tension by asserting that choices to violate basic rights represented not rational consent but wicked licentiousness, and by simply avoiding extensive analysis of potential conflicts between consent and individual rights.[60] Most pertinently, he never considered whether the refusal of an existing citizenry to consent to the membership of a new applicant, or to sustain consent to the citizenship of an existing member, might in some circumstances represent a violation of that individual's natural rights. Locke's orientation toward protection of individual human rights suggests that he would argue that communities should ordinarily be quite inclusive in admitting new members and maintaining existing memberships. Nevertheless, the logic of Locke's formulation of the social contract doctrine, like Rousseau's, indicated that consent to membership must indeed be mutual, granted by the representatives of the existing citizenry as well as by the prospective citizen. Hence his view, as much as the republicans', implicitly sanctioned the permissibility, if not the desirability, of restrictive membership policies, at least so long as those restrictions did not amount to active violations of one's natural rights. Such violations would be difficult to establish, since for Locke, no claims of "natural" civic membership were credible.

Nature and Duration of Obligations of Membership

Locke argued that the principle of consent implied that the obligations of both subject and sovereign were limited. The subject owed obedience to the sovereign only so long as the sovereign honored the social contract, including its guarantees of respect for natural rights. Locke expected that if the sovereign occasionally failed to discharge his obligations due to poor judgment or ill fortune, the subject would bear with him. But in words later echoed by the Declaration of Independence, Locke argued that a "long train of abuses" by the sovereign endangering the rights of the subjects and violating the social contract would justify resistance.[61] As just noted, Locke said little about the reverse issue—whether a state, having decided that a subject had abrogated the social contract, could terminate his membership in the political society through denationalization.[62] Again, Locke's emphasis on protecting personal freedoms, as well as his view of government as simply a subordinate social agent created by the social contract, appears to argue against any extensive governmental power to denationalize members. He did not, however, explicitly rule out such a power.[63]

It was when he addressed the related question of an individual's right to expatriate himself that Locke was forced to recognize that consensual membership could create difficulties. If individuals could relinquish their political subjectship whenever they wished, then the state was always in danger of losing its members through unilateral expatriation, probably at the very times it needed them most, such as during periods of war or economic emergency. Locke tried to meet this problem without departing from purely consensual citizenship, but without great success. He maintained that anyone who gave *express* consent to a commonwealth was "perpetually and indispensably obliged to be and remain unalterably a Subject to it."[64] Locke did not discuss, however, why express consent was irrevocable, nor did he attempt to square this argument with his earlier effort to legitimate the "Examples so frequent in History" in which men had withdrawn from one jurisdiction and set up new governments elsewhere.[65]

He sought to preserve the consent principle in part by maintaining that those who had given only *tacit* consent owed allegiance to their government only so long as they possessed land under it. If they sold their land, they were free to join "any other Commonwealth."[66] Locke might have argued that all earlier expatriates had only tacitly consented to membership and had properly relinquished their land before departing. Indeed, his notion that children consented tacitly to civic membership by claiming their inheritance suggests that most subjects after the founding generation were members only by tacit consent. But if this were so, the requirement of perpetual allegiance from those who had given express consent would probably result in too few such members to withstand widespread unilateral expatriation by others. In any event, Locke did not explain why express consent should be so much more binding than tacit consent. Here, Locke seemed uneasy about pursuing the full implications of purely consensual citizenship; in the end, he felt obliged to invoke a new version of perpetual allegiance, now concealed in the language of consent, as a philosophical deus ex machina.

Political Membership and Rival Memberships

Locke, like the ascriptive theorists, could not adequately harmonize his basic ideal with the claims of rival human attachments and communities. Committed to the primacy of natural liberty, individual rights, and personal choices of membership over all inherited and ascribed commitments and identities, Locke still wished to preserve a place for the sometimes inconsistent claims of parentage and of nation. Thus, as we have seen, he extended the traditional belief in the natural status of the family, claiming greater autonomy for it against the state, which he now portrayed as possessing only artificial, limited authority. Locke also tried to salvage some form of indissoluble political obligation.

But the far more striking feature of his consensualism is that it eroded all claims of authority other than individual consent. The family became almost a transitional institution, preparing children for virtually complete independence from their parents. Despite its considerable autonomy, it was still subject to state intervention, like any other social institution, if its members violated the natural law that the government had been authorized to enforce. But the state could claim no authority over individuals simply because they happened to be attached to it by an accident of nature. Its authority stemmed from, and was limited by, the terms of their consent. At bottom, Locke was ambivalent about all strong particularistic ties, especially powerful national-istic sentiments. They were legitimate as human preferences but might be exploited to deny individuals' freedom of choice or otherwise to justify violations of the natural rights that all possessed.[67]

Thus, the consensual principle potentially undermined all social institutions' claims to legitimate power. In Locke, that potential was muted. But in the late eighteenth century, radical Enlightenment philosophers, especially William Godwin, pushed consensualism to its full logical extreme. For Godwin, the consensual principle was not only incon-sistent with ascriptive political membership, as Locke had argued; more importantly (and, for Godwin, desirably), it completely destroyed the nation's authority, sundered the social contract, and virtually extinguished familial obliga-tions. In his *Enquiry concerning Political Justice*, Godwin reiterated Locke's rebuttal of traditional ascriptive views.[68] He then argued, more pointedly than had Locke, that a child had no obligation to the established government until he "assent[s] to it," scorning any derivation of such an obli-gation from "the contract into which my father entered before I was born." Godwin then proceeded, however, to turn the consent principle against Locke himself.[69]

Godwin first attacked Locke's distinction between tacit and express consent, insisting that acquiescence in a gov-

ernment "is frequently nothing more than a choice on the
part of the individual of what he deems the least evil," or
else it simply reflects people's inability to leave.[70] It is not
approbation. Why, moreover, should even express consent
create perpetual obligations? If a citizen changed his mind
"even an hour" later, his political allegiance and membership could no longer be said to be founded on his consent.
Godwin insisted:

> There is but one power to which I can yield a heart-
> felt obedience, the decision of my own understanding,
> the dictate of my own conscience. . . . What we most
> expect and require in a member of the same com-
> munity is the qualities of a man, and the conduct that
> ought to be observed indifferently by a native or a
> stranger. . . . A promise of allegiance is a declaration
> that I approve the actual constitution of things, and,
> so far as it is binding, an engagement that I will con-
> tinue to support that constitution. But I shall support
> it for as long a time, and in as great a degree, as I
> approve of it. . . . An engagement for anything further
> than this is both immoral and absurd.[71]

If consent was the sole source of legitimacy and obligation, government could truly be legitimate only insofar as
individuals actually and continually affirmed it. In Godwin's
view, there could be no legitimate limits to individual self-
expatriation. The nation's claims of membership were literally "nothing"; they bound the native no more than the
alien—that is, only insofar as the individual accepted them.
Indeed, Godwin hoped that enlightenment would eventually
dispel "the mysteries of government" so that men would
view their countries with a "sense of impartiality"; irra-

tional, emotional "loyalty shall decay." Nor was the family any more sacrosanct. Refusing to grant it any natural authority, Godwin treated the family, so far as the child was concerned, as simply an instrument for his education, to be honored only so far and so long as it was useful.[72]

Advantages and Disadvantages

Locke and Godwin together reveal the attractions and limits of the consent principle. Its attractions are considerable: indeed, leading contemporary writers on citizenship and international law insist even more strongly than Lockean Enlightenment and public law writers did that only consent is an appropriate basis for political membership.[73] Consensualism encourages genuine personal commitment and development, permitting affirmation of one's values through voluntary affiliation with others. At the same time, as Michael Walzer has argued, permitting a democratic community the power to shape its own destiny by granting or refusing its consent to new members is essential if the community is to be able to protect its interests, maintain harmony, and achieve a unifying sense of shared values.[74] When it is combined with liberalism's stress on universally held natural rights, moreover, the consent principle recognizes the aspirations and dignity of all humanity, for it urges a world in which all will be linked politically only by bonds of mutual agreement. Because these values of personal autonomy and communal self-definition are so widely shared in American society today, a morally credible doctrine of civic membership must give central importance to membership based on actual, mutual consent.

But like ascription, consent also poses serious problems. Although some of these problems can be resolved or minimized without great difficulty, others are more troubling. First, of course, there is a problem of proof. Especially after the fact, it will often be hard to determine who has and has not consented to membership in a particular regime, expressly or tacitly.

Second, there is a problem of unjust exclusion. As even Godwin accepted, consent to membership must be mutual, expressed by the existing community as well as by the individual; otherwise, existing members will be coerced and their free choices nullified. But this requirement might imply that a society could deny outsiders opportunities for membership in ways that are harshly restrictive or discriminatory. It might also mean that a society could freely denationalize citizens against their will, reducing their security and status, perhaps even leaving them stateless. In both these instances, adherence to consent may well violate liberalism's other deep commitment to insuring that the basic human rights of all be secured as fully as possible. As noted above, the tension between government by consent and full protection for inalienable rights, visible in liberal theory almost from its inception, is dramatically evident if a democratic government denies all obligation to those who are compelled to turn to it but who are not admitted to be its citizens.

This difficulty points in turn to a third, related problem. The notion of consent is far from being a self-defining concept; it necessarily requires assumptions about several highly controversial questions, such as the scope of free will, the nature of informed choice, and the availability of alternatives. By relying upon notions such as tacit agreement, as we shall see, it may even smuggle in elements of ascription. In the context of consensual citizenship, moreover, the requirement of mutuality may seem to render individual consent hollow in practice because those to whom a state refuses consent may have no practical option to go elsewhere. Persons faced with a choice of only limited, exceedingly harsh alternatives may be more aptly described as compelled than free to choose;[75] more generally, no clear, unproblematic boundary exists between the realms of consent and coercion.

Fourth, there is a problem of unlimited expatriation. As Godwin demonstrated, the consensual principle in its purest form is literally anarchical, jeopardizing all memberships and allegiances. Although Godwin would insist that rational individuals could recognize the imprudence of promoting social instability, political societies probably could not survive if their citizens felt free to renounce their memberships unilaterally whenever it seemed convenient to do so.

Godwin's optimism in this regard indicates a fifth problem of pure consensualism, its narrow, dessicated rationalism. By limiting moral obligations only to those incurred by rational choice, it denies the validity of widespread beliefs that individuals owe something to their family, community, state, and other social groups, and that these groups owe something to their members. The reality of these affective attachments calls into question the adequacy of basing obligation on rational consent alone.

One argument emphasizing such nonvolitional sources of obligation is particularly significant: the insistence that territoriality is of crucial importance for determining the scope of governmental responsibility and the validity of claims to political membership. The principle of territoriality can be seen as ascriptive in that it makes the fact of one's place of residence, which is often a contingent circumstance, central to determining civic membership. But while in Anglo-American law territoriality has indeed most often figured in arguments that take Coke's ascriptive view as their starting point, its ascriptive aspect can be defended by appealing not to any presumed natural order but simply to the realities of existing national authorities and actual, interdependent communities. Territoriality has long been treated as vital for defining governmental authority and nationality because national governments in fact *claim* to exercise authority and responsibility over certain areas. Within those areas, therefore, it is presumptively the duty of the relevant government to exercise jurisdiction over, and take responsibility for, all who are present there. Territoriality consequently has value from the perspective of international law in defining clearly which state has responsibility for a given individual at a given time. Because it insures that all persons can claim protection from the government that most directly asserts power over them, territoriality also resonates to human rights concerns.[76]

Furthermore, attention to territoriality seems justified by the reality that persons within a given territory must inevitably and intensively interact with and affect one another, thereby creating a common life that ordinarily shapes their interests. Hence, defining political membership territorially expresses a recognition that all persons who share a specific locale over a period of time form an organic community, regardless of their inherited legal statuses. If, as many contemporary theorists maintain, moral philosophy should be-

gin with the shared experiences and values of such organic
communities, rather than with more abstract legal or human rights, then it is arguable that the mere fact of presence
in a territory creates a moral claim to citizenship in its
governing polity—a claim that strengthens as the individual's presence lengthens.[77] Of course, this argument from
actual, shared organic community is strained when it is
applied to newly born infants; it has most force on behalf
of those who have grown up in a polity. Even then, such
an argument is not easily made out, for the presence of
some persons in violation of the polity's laws, however pro-
longed, still seems more a violation than an expression of
that community's values; an insistence that they be granted
citizenship obviously represents an ascriptive infringement
of the community's democratic authority to shape its own
destiny.

Of course, a community may have tacitly encouraged the
long-term residence of some aliens that it has never openly
accepted, and its humanitarian values may lead it to place
great weight on the fact that such residence has become a
vital part of those persons' lives. We shall argue later that
such considerations may justify certain sorts of rights and
assistance to aliens, including offering citizenship to many
of America's current illegal alien population, but that they
do not support abandoning efforts to discourage illegal entry
in the future. Generally, however, the case for letting mere
territorial presence qualify one for civic membership cannot
be reconciled with considerations of political self-
determination.

Both the ascriptive and consent principles are thus attractive and problematic in their pure forms. It is tempting,
then, to think that the best features of each can be integrated

into a coherent law of citizenship without sacrificing some values that we cherish. Doubtless, that hope explains why American law has combined the two and has varied the mix of ascriptive and consensual elements—especially of birthright citizenship and the right of expatriation—over time. But, as we shall see in chapters 2, 3 and 4, American law has never adequately reconciled these elements; no combination of consent or ascription that is either theoretically satisfying or practically efficacious, especially in light of current conditions, has yet been achieved. This failure not only represents a deep confusion in American thought about the meaning of political identity; it is also limiting the law's ability to deal effectively with important new challenges to immigration policy.

Except in the intoxicating, sometimes dangerous realm of pure theory, we can never wholly eliminate the tension between our competing national commitments—to political membership based on mutual consent and to transcendent human rights that an ascriptive birthright citizenship, designed in earlier days for quite different purposes, has helped to protect. Like other enduring dualities in political life—that between order and liberty, for example—this tension reflects fundamental, ultimately irreducible value conflicts. Nevertheless, we believe that the law can hope to reconcile the competing values better than it does at present; for those committed to both individual liberties and consensual government, the most desirable policy is one in which majoritarian choice is exercised in practice to secure basic human rights and interests. This goal leads us to propose, in chapter 5, a more consensual citizenship law, a more inclusive immigration law, and a more effective enforcement policy.

2

THE AMERICAN LAW OF CITIZENSHIP PRIOR TO THE FOURTEENTH AMENDMENT

American law has in fact embodied ascriptive and consensual elements from its earliest days. At birth, the new American state inherited two legal traditions concerning political membership: the English common law, expounded above all by Sir William Blackstone,[1] and continental public law, expounded by Hugo Grotius[2] and Samuel Puffendorf[3] but subsequently elaborated by the Swiss writers Jean-Jacques Burlamaqui[4] and Emmerich de Vattel.[5] Although each tradition embraced certain aspects of both the ascriptive and consensual principles, the common law emphasized the ascriptive view of Coke and Filmer, while the public-law treatises increasingly bore strong Lockean influences. Through the antebellum period, American statesmen and judges, confronted with a choice between conflicting traditions, generally adopted the common-law view. This choice, however, was controversial and hedged about with important exceptions. In dealing with the question of expatriation and the treatment of Indians and blacks, legislators and judges increasingly confined the common-law understanding of birthright citizenship by drawing upon consensualist doctrines grounded in the public law tradition. They thereby demonstrated both the liberating and the repressive potential of the consent principle.

By the eighteenth century, even the common law had begun to reflect the new Lockean emphasis on consent as the basis of civic membership. Blackstone, for instance, repeated the common-law view that: "Natural allegiance is such as is due from all men born within the king's dominions immediately upon their birth. For, immediately upon their birth they are under the king's protection; at a time, too, when (during their infancy) they are incapable of protecting themselves. Natural allegiance is therefore a debt of gratitude; which cannot be forfeited, cancelled, or altered, by any change of time, place, or circumstance. . . . " But Blackstone immediately added, "nor by anything but the united concurrence of the legislature."[6] Unlike Coke, he could not accept that even the mutual consent of subject and sovereign could not dissolve the political bond. Blackstone thus propelled the movement toward a consensual theory of civic membership.[7]

The most important of the later public-law theorists, Burlamaqui and Vattel, went further and rejected birthright subjectship and perpetual allegiance altogether. Indeed, both of them articulated consensual principles that, while remaining within a Lockean framework, went beyond his views concerning the state's obligation to preserve family unity, the requirements of the social contract concerning children's political membership, the nature of tacit consent, the power of the state to exclude aliens, and rights of denationalization and expatriation. These innovations rendered consensualism more practical and consistent, although they failed to resolve all of the theoretical difficulties found in Locke and Godwin.

Burlamaqui echoed Locke in the distinction he drew between express and tacit consent, his belief in the natural authority of the family but not the state, his imputation of tacit consent from children's willingness to remain in their parents' community at the age of maturity, and his insistence that this consent not be understood simply as a refusal to throw off a membership acquired through place of birth. Burlamaqui began to depart from Locke, however, in holding that children did acquire a kind of provisional political membership at birth. The children of parents residing within a sovereign's community of allegiance, he argued, enjoyed the right to be treated as members until they reached majority, and were then entitled to join the parents' state if they wished.

The assignment of any sort of membership at birth, even a provisional one, constituted in a sense an acceptance of a mild form of ascription. This acceptance was probably motivated by the impracticality of Locke's refusal to recognize any civic status for children until their maturity. To Burlamaqui, however, this concession to ascription was more apparent than real, for he thought that this provisional membership could be derived from consensualist premises. He argued that the rights he ascribed to the children of citizens followed from the supposition that the parents had obtained those guarantees from the state earlier, as tacit conditions of their own membership. Like Vattel and other subsequent public-law writers, Burlamaqui maintained that the implicit social contract upon which all just states rested their sovereign authority must be hypothesized to contain assurances of the option of citizenship for the children of the polity's members. Given the preeminent importance of family unity to most persons, individuals would not conceivably agree to join a political community without being assured that their offspring would be eligible to belong to it as well. For this reason, Burlamaqui, while acknowledging that this guarantee was only an assumption based on social contractarian reasoning rather than an explicit provision in positive law, regarded it as simply too fundamental to be denied.[8]

Hence the birthright status of children stemmed from consensual agreements between the state and those citizens most entitled to speak for the children until they could speak for themselves—their parents. Burlamaqui also appeared to assume that all individuals legally admitted into a community, resident aliens as well as citizens, had obtained these rights for their offspring upon entering. He added that it was *only* because choice of residence at maturity amounted to tacit consent that a sovereign had "no occasion to tender the oath of allegiance to the children who are afterwards born in his dominion."[9]

While sharing Locke's reticence concerning denationalization of citizens, Burlamaqui went beyond him to assert that any subject, however his membership had been acquired, could terminate that membership by going to settle elsewhere. The sovereign's permission to expatriate was normally required, he argued, but a commitment to personal liberty meant that the sovereign should grant permission unless "very important reasons," such as military necessity, counseled otherwise. Ultimately, however, Burlamaqui, like

Locke, remained equivocal about expatriation, calling the right of removal "inherent in all free peoples," yet also insisting that citizens were bound by their own consent to obey whatever emigration laws existed in their state.[10]

Vattel, writing somewhat later in the eighteenth century, also strongly affirmed consensual membership, but with a slightly different emphasis. According to the "law of nature," which he understood to be the law of perfect reason and justice, "children follow the condition of their fathers . . . it is not naturally the place of birth that gives rights, but extraction."[11] Vattel made it clear that (whatever its original motivations) he defended the rule of *jus sanguinis* only because it was, despite its ascriptive aspect, the most realistic way to approximate membership by consent, given that children were unable to consent for themselves until their maturity. Like Burlamaqui, he thus unequivocally rejected membership by birth and argued that society should provisionally treat children as sharing the political membership of their fathers; the father was again understood to have demanded an opportunity for his children to share his political identity as a condition of his own consent to membership.[12] Both writers, then, not only rooted membership in consent alone but reinforced the Lockean deference to familial unity. Vattel, however, went furthest in defining the rights of the child with reference to the father's status, for he held that the children of permanent residents were guaranteed only the option of becoming permanent residents themselves; they did not have to be offered full citizenship.[13]

Vattel then extended Locke's and Burlamaqui's claim that one's choice to reside in the parents' society at maturity amounted to tacit consent. All persons could "renounce their right" to membership in that community, he maintained, if they simply found the membership inconvenient, "of no advantage." They should make some return for what they had previously received from their polity, including education and protection, perhaps through customs payments. But this obligation, while genuine, was not so great as to justify overriding their natural freedom.[14] If they remained, however, they were taken to have tacitly consented to give allegiance.

Vattel also followed Burlamaqui, if not Locke, in defending an ongoing right of expatriation. So long as his society had "no real need" of him, a citizen was entitled to withdraw from it. He could not, however, properly expatriate himself to escape military service or other special obligations, such as criminal prosecution or a public debt. Vattel cited circumstances in which a citizen's natural rights gave him an "absolute right" to expatriation, such as when his government had violated the social contract or when he could not support himself in his homeland. A "good citizen," however, would not leave his country without "very strong reasons"; like Burlamaqui, Vattel argued that citizens should respect their nation's emigration laws, so long as the restrictions did not amount to permanent enslavement of them.[15]

Vattel also followed the consensual principle's logic of mutuality more consistently than Burlamaqui or Locke by explicitly recognizing unilateral governmental powers to denationalize citizens, as well as to deny admission to foreigners, along with his affirmation of the individual's right of self-expatriation. Unlike his predecessors, Vattel argued

that the state was entitled to exile or banish a member
permanently, thereby ending its authority over him. While
these forms of denationalization could be punitive, neither
required an actual criminal act as a precondition.[16]

Vattel also held that no other nation had an absolute duty
to admit those who had left their homelands due to exile,
banishment, or some other pressing cause. Here, however,
he was forced to face the conflict between a nation's consensual power of self-determination and his liberal belief
in human rights. Vattel accepted that those driven from
their homelands by exile or some other calamity had a natural right to seek residence elsewhere, and in this regard
he denied that property rights could justify refusing ne-
cessities to those in need.[17] At the same time, he diluted
this position by terming this right to dwell elsewhere "imperfect," meaning that it did not include a right to constrain
those who refused to honor it. Vattel viewed the right as
"imperfect" because, although duties of humanity implied
that refuge should not be denied lightly, the "natural liberty"
of each nation nonetheless gave it the authority "to judge,
whether it is, or is not in a proper situation to receive this
stranger." Vattel hoped the basis of refusal would not be
"groundless and frivolous fears" and that "charity and com-
miseration" would guide national choices. But if permission
to enter and join were denied, even for inadequate reasons,
outsiders had no recourse but moral disapprobation.[18]

Similarly, Vattel was aware of the potential conflict between national security and the extensive right of self-expatriation that he endorsed. Like his predecessors, he
therefore argued that positive laws restricting individual
expatriation should generally be followed. And, like them,

he stressed that enduring memberships in particular societies were instinctual and natural; in contrast to Godwin's
universalism, Vattel even praised "love of our country."[19]

Yet also like Locke, neither Vattel nor Burlamaqui succeeded in defining principled limits to their consensualism.
Neither considered the extent to which cultural homogeneity
might be necessary in order for societies based on consensual membership to endure. While Vattel's doctrines on
denationalization and expatriation were the most consistent, they permitted harsh exclusions by the state and such
broad personal latitude to expatriate that he felt compelled
to exhort citizens to maintain existing allegiances, even as
he exhorted states to be generous to outsiders. He also conceded that a society might reject his natural law views on
both birthright citizenship and expatriation so long as they
did not work grievous injustices.[20] Hence his consensualism,
too, entailed difficulties that were obvious even to its author.

The American Revolution was fought to secure inalienable
rights and to establish government by consent of the governed; it sought to create a liberal republic of self-governing
citizens in place of monarchical rule over subjects. It is not
surprising, therefore, that the consensual view of political
membership was extremely prominent in early American
political thought. The Declaration of Independence itself
was a Lockean justification of expatriation; it argued that
the British monarch, not the American people, had broken
the social contract by exceeding the limits of his legitimate
authority through denials of representation and violations
of basic rights. Furthermore, a liberal consensualist dismissal of the claims of particular, accidental memberships,
including nationality, was visible in the thought of some of

the leading revolutionaries, including, ironically, the new
nation's patriarch, George Washington. Espousing Christian
and liberal principles of universal human worth, Washington was uncomfortable with fervent national chauvinism,
even on behalf of the United States.[21]

America's early statesmen, however, appear to have been
quite sensitive to the difficulties of a purely consensual citizenship, for in practice they perpetuated legal doctrines
reflecting Blackstone's slightly liberalized ascriptive view. In
the most important example, the framers of the Constitution
indicated that they presumed that the native-born were
citizens by birth. Thus, although they left the status of citizenship undefined,[22] they adopted, without recorded debate, the requirements that the president be a "natural-
born Citizen," or "a Citizen" at the time the Constitution
was ratified.[23] Such language clearly implied that citizenship
would be acquired by birth, even if it left unspecified the
circumstances of birth that made infants "natural-born"
citizens.[24]

In certain respects, of course, the new nation's citizenship
laws did embody consensualist premises. Alexander Hamilton argued in the *Federalist Papers* that the new Constitution rested American government as a whole even more
firmly on "the solid basis of THE CONSENT OF THE PEOPLE,"
which he termed the "pure, original fountain of all legitimate authority."[25] The Constitution accordingly assigned
the federal government the power to grant or to deny the
citizenry's consent to the immigration and naturalization
of new members. From the start, these powers were used
to enforce the republic's sense of what it wanted to be and
to become, a sense that always involved some harsh exclu-

sions from citizenship. These were explicitly advocated and defended by appeal to the republican insistence on the community's power and duty to maintain unity, identity, and homogeneity through denial of consent to the membership of those who seemed too different from the existing populace.

Thomas Jefferson, for example, argued against encouraging the immigration of the "servile masses of Europe" on the ground that they would transform the "homogeneous" and "peaceable" American people into a "heterogeneous, incoherent, distracted mass" unfit for republican self-government.[26] (Jefferson was, however, sufficiently liberal to believe that citizenship should be granted to those who nevertheless came.) When the new nation came to consider its first naturalization laws in the 1790s, numerous concerns were expressed that foreigners might be too unfamiliar with republican institutions to make it wise to permit them citizenship without a long period of residency. The examples of Greece, Rome, and Switzerland were invoked to show that, because republican "character" was hard to form, healthy republics "jealously guarded their citizenship."[27] As a result, the early laws did include waiting periods of fluctuating lengths, the republican requirement that applicants give up any aristocratic titles, and a requirement of racial homogeneity, the exclusion of all non-whites from eligibility for naturalization. Those restrictions somewhat blunted the significance of the fact that the nation set no limits on immigration until the late nineteenth century. Subsequently, as we shall see, American citizenship law embraced the ascriptive common-law view much more than the consensualist public tradition. Moreover, it was, regrettably, usually exclusionary racial concerns that led courts to stress

instead the community's consensualist power to admit or
deny new members, as with Indians and blacks, and that
led Congress eventually to adopt immigration restrictions.

Four elements go far toward explaining why late eigh-
teenth- and early nineteenth-century Americans resisted the
full-blown liberal consensualism professed in the Declaration of Independence, either by reaffirming the ascriptive
understanding of birthright citizenship explicitly or by evad-
ing specification of the nature of American citizenship. First,
during the Revolution, the new American states wanted to
claim the allegiance of all native-born inhabitants and to
prosecute and seize the property of those who supported
Great Britain. Hence, they asserted that it was treason for
anyone born in the colonies to adhere to the British side,
and they confiscated Tory landholdings.[28] No other policy
seemed safe if they were to succeed in their precarious cause.
Subsequently, the logic of their own revolution compelled
Americans to recognize it instead as a period during which
individuals had possessed a "right of election" to affirm
allegiance to either the British or the American cause.[29]
Property claims were largely settled by the postwar treaties,
in which the United States agreed to recognize the prewar
American property holdings of British subjects.[30] But many
American judges still found it more expedient, if not more
consistent, to confine the right of election to a relatively
short period of revolutionary chaos, and to view persons as
obligated to their governments both before and after this
period in ways that they could not unilaterally alter.[31]

Second, the American colonies, and later the states, vig-
orously sought to attract new inhabitants who would help
construct the new society, and birthright citizenship was

viewed as an incentive for young families to immigrate here. This meant, of course, that American-born children of aliens often possessed dual citizenship because their parents' country of origin viewed them as following the nationality of their parents. That difficulty, however, was then of slight concern.[32]

Third, the doctrines of birthright citizenship, perpetual allegiance, and expatriation raised sensitive questions about whether state or national citizenship was primary in the new constitutional system, questions that no one wished to confront squarely by exploring how far American citizenship was ascriptive or consensually based. Did birth within the United States mean that all states had to accord the individual full state citizenship? Could a state expatriate a person, stripping him either of state citizenship or both state and United States citizenship? As James Kettner has argued, resolution of such questions turned upon the relationship of state and national authority, a matter so politically charged that American courts were cautious about deciding questions, especially expatriation, that involved not only choices between ascriptive and consensual views, but also engendered federal–state and sectional confrontations.[33]

Finally, many early nineteenth-century American courts also worried that rejection of birthright citizenship would imply an unlimited right of expatriation. They believed, as even enthusiasts of consensual citizenship such as Locke and his public-law followers feared, that such a right would place government in jeopardy. American judges repeatedly invoked the spectre of soldiers on the battlefield renouncing their allegiance to dramatize the possible danger.[34]

Yet despite these powerful incentives either to endorse

the doctrine of birthright citizenship explicitly or to avoid
issues involving consensual challenges to it, American law
was unable to adhere unequivocally to the common-law
rule for two sharply contrasting reasons. First, Americans
were devoutly committed to the principle of consensual
government and to the right of expatriation. Failure to recognize that right in law seemed to render the rhetoric of
the Revolution hollow and hypocritical. Moreover, there were
strong immediate motives to uphold a consensually defended right of expatriation, for the British continued to
claim the perpetual allegiance of their former American
subjects, and to impress them into the Royal Navy, well into
the nineteenth century.[35]

Second, Americans wanted to assert authority over Indians and native-born blacks, but they did not want to admit
them to birthright citizenship. The public-law tradition,
particularly Vattel, provided arguments, based on the requirement that a society consent to new members, that
could be used to justify discriminatory exclusions, and
American courts relied heavily on them. Thus, by the Civil
War, American law contained several exceptions to the common-law rule of birthright citizenship.

Expatriation

The expatriation question produced the most direct clash
between the ascriptive and the consensual views. Since even
the public-law treatise writers thought native-born children
should be treated as citizens, albeit provisionally, the ques-

tion of the basis of membership usually did not arise until an adult sought to expatriate himself.

Then the issue could not easily be avoided. At a minimum, Americans felt compelled to accept that expatriation could occur when the social contract was broken, as during the Revolution, or when the sovereign and the subject mutually consented to it, as even Blackstone had held.[36] But many were unwilling to go further toward consensualism than this. The public-law writers' view of birthright citizenship as only provisional, and as attached not to the child directly but to the parent as a condition of his own membership, was usually acknowledged to constitute a more genuinely consensual view of citizenship. But although this position still permitted the state to regulate expatriation, its liberal, volitional focus suggested that the state could not deny that right without compelling reasons, and that even those reasons could be overridden in the name of individual natural rights of life and liberty. Thus, the logic of the consensual public-law view implied a more robust right of expatriation than many American officials were prepared to embrace.

While memories of the Revolution remained fresh, the Supreme Court did sometimes suggest expansive views of expatriation. Thus, in *Talbot* v. *Jansen*, a 1795 case, all parties conceded that the doctrine of perpetual allegiance was illiberal and irrational, that "birth gives no property in the man," so that he should not be "compelled to continue in a society to which he is accidentally attached, when he can better his station elsewhere."[37] On the facts of this case, however, the Court decided that Talbot, a privateer who was claiming French naturalization so as to avoid American laws banning his activities, had not properly expatriated himself but had only engaged in illegal acts under the cover of foreign citizenship.[38]

In subsequent cases decided by Federalist judges, the courts increasingly held instead that, apart from a period of election during the Revolution, the common-law doctrine of perpetual allegiance, alterable only by mutual consent, had been and remained binding in American law. Jeffersonian newspapers denounced the claim of a "birth duty of allegiance" as a "fraud upon infancy."[39] But without an expatriation statute, which federalism considerations made infeasible, any broad right of expatriation seemed to make allegiance and property more uncertain than the new nation could tolerate. Thus, while some state courts continued to endorse the sort of broad expatriation right defended in the public-law treatises, federal courts increasingly denied that any such right existed without the explicit consent of Congress.[40]

The expatriation question was also repeatedly considered by the political branches, largely because of the ongoing impressment controversy with Great Britain. The official position varied with diplomatic considerations, but it generally asserted a strong right of expatriation.[41] Even several Supreme Court decisions taking a dim view of voluntary expatriation nonetheless employed reasoning that could be used both to support that right and to challenge birthright citizenship. As noted, the Court accepted the doctrine of a right of election during the Revolution, though without precisely defining its boundaries; in regard to this elective period, at least, it endorsed principles governing parental authority over childrens' political membership much like those of Locke, Burlamaqui, and Vattel.

In *Inglis* v. *Sailor's Snug Harbour*,[42] for example, Justice Joseph Story, reasoning on the assumption that Inglis was a minor at the time of the Revolution, held him to have been incapable therefore of "making an election for himself" during this period. At maturity, Inglis was understood as having "adopted and ratified the choice made for him by his father," since he had not signified "any dissent to the election made for him."[43] This reasoning clearly echoed the public-law view that, at least during America's period of election when the common-law rule of perpetual allegiance did not apply, the child was bound by the parent's choice, but only provisionally, only until he was capable of deciding for himself. The fact that Story looked to the public-law tradition, if only for the revolutionary period, indicates that he agreed that it embodied the requirements of natural law (though he thought positive law could legitimately order otherwise). Story similarly indicated in other contexts that when positive municipal law did not apply, the law of nature, as described by the public-law writers, should be followed.[44] Nonetheless, the willingness of Story and American jurists generally to apply the natural-law doctrines of Vattel and Burlamaqui to the period of election did not alter the courts' commitment to sustaining the common-law rule of birthright citizenship for all other periods.

Oddly, although children born in America of alien parents were generally assumed to be citizens who possessed all the rights and obligations of that status, no court seems to have decided a case directly on the question until *Lynch* v. *Clarke*, a New York case decided in 1844.[45] The decision turned on whether Julia Lynch, born in New York in 1814 of lawfully admitted, temporarily sojourning alien parents, could inherit property as an American citizen. Her father, Patrick Lynch, had lived from 1814 to 1819 on a New York farm owned by his brother Thomas, but the court viewed Patrick as only temporarily resident because he had often professed his intention to return to Ireland and had never officially declared an intent to become an American citizen as required by congressional naturalization laws.[46] After the death of both Thomas and Patrick Lynch, Julia and Thomas's business partner, John Clarke, contested the claim of her uncle Bernard Lynch to inherit Thomas's mineral waters business and land.

In opposing her claim, Bernard Lynch's lawyers made several arguments. At the heart of their case, however, was an appeal to Vattel's consensual conception of citizenship rather than to the common-law principle of ascriptive perpetual allegiance. They maintained that birthright citizenship, together with perpetual allegiance, were products of the "darkened ages" of English "tyranny," and so were "unfit for a free and just nation to adopt."[47] They insisted, therefore, that where the case law provided no clear answer, the court should treat the situation as Story had treated the absence of positive law in revolutionary times—by appealing to the abstract justice of public-law principles.[48] They further argued that Chancellor Kent's precept, that under American law "natives were all persons born within the jurisdiction of the United States," should be taken as presupposing, with Burlamaqui and Vattel, "that the parents are themselves citizens, so as to be in a situation to give the

child the benefits of their own political condition."[49] Moreover, although Congress had not directly addressed the question, it had passed numerous naturalization statutes
indicating that the children of alien parents became citizens
when their parents were naturalized, while failing explicitly
to distinguish between native-born and foreign-born children of alien parents.

Bernard Lynch's lawyers also argued that Congress's silence on the question of whether native-born aliens had
rights beyond those of the foreign-born should be taken as
a decision to leave the issue "where the policy and reason
of public law had settled it, unaffected by statutory regu-
lation."[50] Here again, they maintained, the doctrines of Burlamaqui and Vattel should be applied. The lawyers conceded
that Congress might merely have expected the courts to deal
with questions of civic membership on an individual, case-
by-case basis, but they denied that it could ever have meant
them to employ the feudal principles of the common law
for American citizenship questions.[51]

The lawyers defending Julia Lynch's claim to citizenship,
on the other hand, pointed out that on the related issue of
expatriation, American courts had leaned to the common
law, not to Vattel. They argued that the common law was
understood to be generally applicable in America, except
where it did not fit American circumstances and rights, and
that Vattel himself had said his "law of nature" did not
apply where there was contrary and nonoppressive municipal law.[52]

Assistant Vice Chancellor Lewis Sandford upheld Lynch's
birthright citizenship, explicitly rejecting the public-law
conception of consensual membership. His opinion pro-

claimed citizenship to be a national right to be decided in accordance with federal law, which incorporated the common law "to a limited extent" as a "system of national jurisprudence."[53] Common-law principles were not to be followed when inappropriate to American circumstances, statutes, and principles, but were relevant whenever federal law was unclear. Congress's silence on the issue of birthright citizenship, Sandford ruled, implied a willingness that the courts follow the common law. Reasoning from various phrases in the naturalization statutes, he concluded that the statutory references to children of aliens referred only to children of aliens born abroad.[54]

Although Sandford found federal law to have adopted the common-law rule, he also maintained that even if the issue had "to be determined solely on its intrinsic propriety and adaptation to our circumstances," the common-law doctrine would be preferable as a matter of policy; it was "plain and simple," meeting the law's need for "fixed, certain, and intelligible rules."[55] Sandford further maintained that although courts had often treated birthright citizenship and expatriation as separate issues (they had been implicitly unanimous on the first issue and closely divided on the second), the issues were in fact related, making abandonment of the birthright rule problematic.[56] He criticized Vattel's suggestion that the law should give to a child of alien parents:

the election, on arriving at maturity, to become a citizen, either of the state where he was born, or of the state of which his father was a member. In effect, this brings us back to the theory of the formation of states and governments, by voluntary compact of their inhabitants; and yields to every man, the unqualified right of throwing off allegiance by birth, whenever he becomes of age, and attaching himself to any community which pleases him. And if he may do it when he attains his full age, why may he not exercise the same natural right, every successive year of his life? And with these notions of allegiance fully established, a state with a well appointed army of its citizens in the field today, might tomorrow find itself without citizens, and its troops in the full fruition of a new allegiance, in the ranks of its enemy.

Sanford briefly added that it would be "unjust" to helpless native-born infants to deny or even delay their citizenship.[57]

For our purposes, what is most interesting about Sandford's opinion is not his rejection of Vattel or his acceptance of the common-law view of citizenship. It is his conclusion that the issue was still unsettled even in 1844, and that the choice between these conceptions of citizenship remained (in the absence of statute) a judicial one, to be made in accordance with the principles that seemed most consistent with America's distinctive circumstances and principles of free government. Sandford's choice of the common-law view was based essentially on the feared practical consequences of purely volitional citizenship—particularly a right of expatriation—for the stability of government.

This consideration, we have seen, had troubled all but the most radical advocates of consensualism, but it aroused little or no concern in the political branches during the first half of the nineteenth century. Indeed, their advocacy of expatriation eventually led to enactment of America's first Expatriation Act within a day of the ratification of the Four-

teenth Amendment. That act was chiefly motivated by a
continuing desire to deny ascriptive-minded foreign governments, especially Great Britain, any authority over those
who chose to become American citizens. It proclaimed expatriation "a natural and inherent right of all people," guaranteed equal protection for naturalized and native-born
citizens, and assigned the president the duty of defending
naturalized citizens against encroaching foreign states.[58]

Given this growing acceptance of the expatriation right
that Sandford and others had feared, it was clearly open to
American judges, at least prior to passage of the Citizenship
Clause of the Fourteenth Amendment, to read even formulations of birthright citizenship that expressed the common-law tradition, such as Chancellor Kent's, in a way that
would vindicate consensual premises. A court need only
advert to the special significance of consent to the American
polity and interpret "birth within the nation's allegiance"
or "jurisdiction" as being restricted to birth to parents who
were themselves legal members of the political community.
The courts, after all, had already added to Blackstone's idea
of mutual consensual termination of birthright citizenship
the Lockean justification of expatriation when the social
contract had been violated. Vattelian assertions of a consensualist interpretation of the status of the native-born,
and of a broader individual right of expatriation, would
only have furthered this evolution.

Like Locke, American courts essentially ignored the other
side of the expatriation issue; they did not consider whether
the community was entitled to withdraw its consent to
membership, denationalizing a citizen.[59] Until the 1880s,
the nation sought to attract citizens, not expel them. The

courts, however, did have to resolve whether the community could deny membership to some native-born persons widely considered unsuited for citizenship, particularly Indians and blacks,[60] and on this issue they repeatedly endorsed the republican and Vattelian belief that a state could indeed refuse to consent to membership or, having previously consented, could withdraw that consent. In doing so, the courts confirmed consensualism's exclusionary, repressive potential.

Indians

The problem of Indians grew increasingly acute as the nineteenth century progressed. Ever more Indians lived within tribes that claimed to be sovereign nations but resided on lands surrounded by states and territories over which the United States asserted sovereignty. A number of tribes negotiated treaties with the United States that permitted individual Indians to become citizens if they left the tribe and merged with the white population.[61] Otherwise, Indians were ineligible for naturalization, and while residing in the tribes, they were understood to owe primary allegiance to their tribal government. Located amidst lands that the federal government regarded as its own, those governments were viewed by the United States as separate but not truly independent political entities. They survived essentially at the sufferance of the American government, as dependent peoples subject to its power and protection.[62]

For those who wished to deny citizenship to Indians, that status made adherence to the traditional common-law understanding of birthright citizenship impossible. Coke had, after all, argued in *Calvin's Case* that any measure of protection provided a child at birth sufficed to render him a natural subject, regardless of the nationality of his parents. If the Indian tribes were subject to the protection of the United States, as the government insisted, then obviously their infants were recipients of at least minimal protection. And if birthright citizenship was merely a continuation of the common-law status of birthright subjectship, then those infants were native-born citizens of the United States.

To reject that inexorable logic of the ascriptive view, American jurists found support in the public-law tradition. Notably, in *Goodell v. Jackson*, an 1823 case, even Chancellor James Kent, who otherwise defended the common-law rule of birthright political membership, looked to the rival tradition to define the status of the son of an Oneida Indian who claimed the right to inherit lands previously granted by the state of New York to his father, a soldier in the Revolutionary War.[63] Kent held that the Indians constituted "dependent tribes, governed by their own usages and chiefs, but placed under our protection, and subject to our coercion." But this did not make them so subordinate to the United States as to constitute them members of the American community. Appealing to Vattel, Kent insisted that a state could be "inferior" to and "restrained" by another without losing its independence and sovereignty "in certain respects." Such inferior states still possessed decisive dominion over those born under the tribal government, so Indians owed allegiance to and were members of their respective tribes, not of the United States.[64]

Kent's opinion was somewhat misleading, for it stressed the ascriptive language of allegiance to the authority with

dominion over the person, in keeping with his endorsement
of the common law's ascriptive view in other contexts. His
argument here, however, made sense only on the basis of
Vattel's consensual understanding of political membership,
not on the common law's ascriptive view. If membership
is a product of a social contract, then it is plausible to say
that a dependent or tributary nation has contractually ceded
only certain aspects of its sovereignty to another state, while
maintaining enough independence so that the law can pre-
sume that children born to its natives are provisionally its
citizens. But if citizenship is ascribed to anyone whom a
sovereign power protects at birth to any extent, then birth
within a protected dependent nation ought to create membership in the community of allegiance of the superior nation as well. Indeed, membership in the dominant nation
should be primary, since its power and protection are ultimately most decisive. Kent dealt with the difficulty raised
by Coke's view that any protection was sufficient to create
birthright allegiance by simply failing to acknowledge it.

This willingness to treat the Indian tribes as being under
the authority of the United States in some circumstances
but not in others was soon imitated by the United States
Supreme Court. In *Cherokee Nation* v. *Georgia*, an 1831 case,
Chief Justice John Marshall argued that the tribes were "domestic dependent nations" amounting to "wards" of the
United States, who looked to its government for protection,
addressing the president as their "great father."[65] Hence,
they were not foreign states entitled to sue a state in the
federal courts. But the following year, in *Worcester* v. *Georgia*, Marshall adopted the position advanced by the dissenters in *Cherokee Nation*: the tribes were tributary states, as

defined by Vattel, under the protection of the United States, but not in a way that involved the "destruction" of their independence.[66] Georgia therefore could not regulate members of the tribe as it would its own citizens, abrogating all tribal authority as it had attempted to do through a series of statutes. Although this result was reassuring to the Cherokees, Marshall's opinion also meant that henceforth Kent's view of the status of Indians would be treated as authoritative throughout the nation. The tribes now possessed the status of Vattel's tributary nations, sufficiently independent that their natives were not members of the American political community, but sufficiently dependent to be subject to federal law.[67]

Blacks

Only one status was better suited than this to facilitate exploitation under the law; that status, of course, was slavery. Blacks presented an even greater problem for the doctrine of birthright allegiance than Indians, for they could not plausibly be held to owe allegiance to any other government, dependent or independent. Black slaves, to be sure, posed no great difficulty: they were ascribed the status of native-born subjects, but their subjectship was absolute, wholly devoid of any rights.[68] In the case of free blacks, however, born entirely within the jurisdiction and under the power and protection of the United States government, it was not apparent how the common-law theory of birthright citizenship could deny them political membership.

The issue first received extensive attention in 1820, when

Congress debated the question of whether admission of Missouri to the Union would violate the Privileges and Immunities Clause of Article IV by denying to free blacks basic rights accorded to other citizens. The proposed Missouri Constitution barred free blacks and mulattoes from entering the state. To resolve the issue, it seemed necessary to decide whether free, native-born blacks could be considered American citizens at all. Numerous representatives maintained that they should be viewed as possessing birthright citizenship equally with whites. Congressman Joseph Hemphill of Pennsylvania, for example, argued that although citizenship had never been formally defined by constitutional or statutory provisions, "if being a native, and free born, and of parents belonging to no other nation or tribe, does not constitute a citizen in this country, I am at a loss to know in what manner citizenship is acquired by birth."[69]

To defeat this powerful ascriptive argument, opponents of citizenship for free blacks relied essentially on two claims. Both were logically vulnerable but practically influential. They argued, first, that no one could be eligible for citizenship unless he was eligible for all of the basic prerogatives of that status. Since most nonslave states denied blacks voting rights and other liberties, they could not be viewed as citizens. Just what rights had to be available in order for one to be a citizen was a matter of controversy. This argument, after all, faced the obvious and insuperable objection that women and children were treated by the law as citizens yet were denied most of the political rights denied to blacks.[70]

The most logically powerful version of this essentially circular argument had to reject the common law's strongly ascriptive view of citizenship and appeal to the public-law understanding of the rights attaching at birth. Representatives Alexander Smyth and Louis McLane each argued that to be born a citizen, one must belong to a class eligible for naturalization, and they cited the public law generally, and Vattel in particular, to maintain that children followed the status of their fathers. Since the fathers of free blacks were, because of their race, ineligible for naturalization under federal law, and since the children inherited that status, they lacked an eligibility that was a prerequisite for citizenship.[71]

A second line of argument against citizenship for free blacks was only hinted at in the Missouri Compromise debates, but it would be developed subsequently by courts and ultimately would be pivotal to Chief Justice Roger B. Taney's opinion in *Dred Scott*. This argument, too, appealed to the public law's consensual understanding of citizenship. It advanced the claim that blacks were not parties to the social contract that created the United States by ratifying the Constitution, and that the United States was therefore a white community until it explicitly decided to become otherwise. Charles Pinckney, who claimed authorship of the Privileges and Immunities Clause, stated that he had not believed blacks were citizens in the American political community at the nation's founding, and that he did not believe any had become so since. United States citizenship was confined to the original white parties to the American social contract, to their descendants, and to those admitted by treaty, naturalization, or native birth to a class eligible for citizenship.[72] The remarks of other members of Congress suggested similar views.[73]

While Missouri won admission, however, many north-
erners remained unconvinced, and the northern states generally came to recognize free, native-born blacks explicitly
as citizens even as they subjected them to extensive political
and civil disabilities.[74] The courts of the southern states
instead became increasingly adamant in their denials that
blacks—freeborn, emancipated, or otherwise—could ever
be citizens. To them, free blacks were "subjects," "deni-
zens," "quasi-citizens," "wards of the state," or some other
contrived "middle" class between slave and citizen.[75] An
1822 Kentucky case, *Amy (a woman of colour)* v. *Smith*,
clearly demonstrated how the southern courts were compelled to deny the common-law view of birthright citizenship to avoid granting free blacks citizenship.[76] The court
maintained that although birth could create citizens as well
as subjects, it "indisputably requires something more to
make a citizen, than it does to make a subject." That something, as indicated in the 1820 congressional debates, was
eligibility for certain rights: "It is, in fact, not the place of
a man's birth, but the rights and privileges he may be entitled to enjoy, which make him a citizen."[77] The rights and
privileges in question, moreover, had to be those of "the
highest class of society." Women, it might be responded,
should therefore obviously not be citizens; the court, however, argued instead that they were "generally dependent
upon adult males" and so should "partake of the quality of
those adult males," including citizenship.[78] This argument
might logically suggest that though free blacks were not
citizens, dependent black slaves were. The court, however,
did not draw that conclusion. Thus on the question of free
blacks, antebellum courts divided sharply, northern ones

affirming the ascriptive common-law view of birthright citizenship and southern ones modifying or rejecting it.

The legal treatment of expatriation, Indians, and black slaves suggests that Americans generally adhered to the ascriptive principle prior to the Fourteenth Amendment, but that they were well aware of the doctrines of the public-law writers and actually followed them in certain contexts. How and when these doctrines were used was determined by considerations of politics and policy, not legal or theoretical consistency. Thus, courts recognized the force of the arguments for consensual citizenship and an accompanying right of expatriation and occasionally endorsed them. On the whole, however, they perpetuated the common-law birthright citizenship rule, primarily out of concern about the problem of unlimited expatriation. Even so, they acknowledged more explicitly than Blackstone or the common law had that political allegiance could be dissolved by sovereign violations of the consensual social contract, as well as by mutual consent. Moreover, American legislators and diplomats repeatedly asserted, and finally wrote into statutory law, the broader Vattelian view of expatriation.[79] In regard to Indians, and blacks too, Vattel's consensual doctrines were employed whenever the state or national governments found the inclusive ascriptive principle inconvenient. Conversely, arguments for the common-law ascriptive view often came to be perpetuated, ironically, by humanitarians who were greatly opposed to nonconsensual feudal doctrines generally but who admired the inclusiveness potentially provided by ascription of citizenship to all at birth.[80]

As the next chapter indicates, American law's use of both

ascriptive and consensual understandings of the birthrights
of the native-born makes it difficult to know precisely what
the framers of the Fourteenth Amendment's Citizenship
Clause had in mind, a difficulty not altogether alleviated by
their debates. It is therefore all the more important to recognize that the American Congress, courts, and statesmen
had always drawn freely on both traditions, selecting among
them largely on grounds of expediency. The result was a
law that sacrificed theoretical consistency for some putative
practical advantages. We shall suggest in chapter 4 that in
today's circumstances, the price we pay for that inconsistency may be increasing as the supposed advantages turn
out to be less compelling and more problematic than they
seemed in the past.

3

THE FOURTEENTH AMENDMENT AND THE 1868 EXPATRIATION ACT

Chief Justice Taney's decision in the *Dred Scott* case[1] immediately propelled the question of the meaning and status of the consent principle to the very center of America's political consciousness. In *Dred Scott*, the Supreme Court held that no American of African descent, whether freeman or slave, could be a United States citizen by birth.[2] In the Court's view, the framers of the Constitution had intended that only individuals who were state citizens at the time the original Constitution was adopted were United States citizens capable of transmitting that status to their descendants. Not only were free blacks not citizens; slaves were not even "persons" entitled to minimal constitutional protection. Instead, they were simply their masters' property, enjoying (as Taney put it) "no rights which the white man was bound to respect."[3]

By making Dred Scott's citizenship turn upon the putative will and intention of the Framers to exclude all blacks from the American political community, Taney seemed to embrace the consensual conception of citizenship, subordinating the conventional ascriptive view. Furthermore, his approach dramatically revealed an aspect of consensualism that is far more significant today than it was in Taney's America of open borders and unrestricted immigration: the requirement that the consent be mutual and reciprocal, running from government to individual as well as from individual to government. His decision, then, reminds us that consent is a two-way street, harboring racist, exclusionary possibilities as well as liberal, inclusive ones.

For present purposes, not to speak of its effect upon the tragic sequel that *Dred Scott* unleashed, it matters not that Taney got his facts wrong concerning the law of citizenship at the time of the Constitution.[4] What matters is that, as noted earlier, the Constitution did not define the criteria for citizenship and that this omission had created a situation in which federal citizenship arguably depended entirely upon state citizenship, thereby making a decision like *Dred Scott* possible. It was in order to repair this defect and overrule *Dred Scott*'s narrow, state-dependent conception of United States citizenship that the Citizenship Clause was adopted.

The framers of the clause, however, did not write on a blank slate. As we have seen, the clause was adopted against a legal and ideological background in which the common-law view of political membership had found acceptance, a view in which (according to Lord Chief Justice Alexander Cockburn, a critic of the common-law rule writing at the time the clause was considered) "a merely casual birth in the country is to have the effect of conferring the character of a British Subject."[5] That view largely reflected its medieval English origins. But the context in which the clause was adopted was strikingly different. America was a more open, less insular society. Its central political ideas were not ascription and allegiance but consent and individual rights.

And the clause was drafted with a very specific purpose in mind. It was designed to elevate to constitutional status the definition of citizenship adopted by statute over President Andrew Johnson's veto only two months earlier and by the very same Congress. A centerpiece of Reconstruction, the Civil Rights Act of 1866[6] had sought to guarantee blacks equal rights, privileges, and immunities under the law. At the same time, it created a new definition of United States citizenship, one that effectively overruled *Dred Scott*: "All persons born in the United States, and not subject to any foreign power, excluding Indians not taxed, are hereby declared to be citizens of the United States."[7]

Although the Citizenship Clause was derived from the 1866 act, it was by no means identical. There were four textual differences. The clause inserted the words "or naturalized" in the definition of citizenship; substituted the phrase "and subject to the jurisdiction thereof" for the phrase "and not subject to a foreign power"; contained no explicit exclusion of Indians (although Section 2 of the Fourteenth Amendment, relating to the formula for apportioning representatives among the states, did, like the 1866 act, exclude "Indians not taxed"); and provided that United States citizens were also citizens "of the State wherein they reside." The legal scholar is sorely tempted to ascribe significance to these intriguing differences in language, especially when they appear in two documents adopted by the same body within a period of weeks. Unfortunately, neither the Congressional debates nor subsequent judicial exegesis provides much insight into the origins or meaning of these textual disparities.

The debates clearly demonstrate, as noted above, that

Congress's purpose in proposing the Fourteenth Amendment immediately after the enactment of the 1866 act was to "constitutionalize" the protections established by the act, including the principle of birthright citizenship. Some doubts had been expressed during the debates on the act concerning Congress's constitutional authority to enact it. These doubts centered upon Congress's power to prohibit discrimination by the states, an objection that President Johnson had emphasized in his veto message.[8] Although the citizenship provision of the act had not been nearly so controversial, some opponents of the bill had contended that Congress's sole constitutional power to confer citizenship was through the enactment of naturalization laws,[9] and that such laws, by definition, could only extend citizenship to the foreign-born. As to persons born here, so the argument went, only a constitutional amendment—presumably one overruling *Dred Scott*—would suffice.[10] Finally, although the Reconstruction Congress had quickly overridden President Johnson's veto, many members were determined to prevent future Congresses and presidents from attempting to dilute the legal protections that the act had extended to the newly freed blacks.[11]

Understanding the amendment's purposes, unfortunately, does not reveal the reasons for the puzzling textual differences between the citizenship provisions of the 1866 act and the amendment. Nevertheless, this understanding, combined with Congress's failure to make much of those differences during debate on the Citizenship Clause, tend to weaken any argument that the clause and the act were animated by fundamentally different motives or principles. This evidence also reduces the danger that, by treating the debates surrounding the act and those surrounding the clause together, we shall do violence to the elusive abstraction known as "congressional intent."

The greatest mystery surrounding the scope of the clause— and for our purposes, the most important question—concerns the meaning of its phrase "and subject to the jurisdiction [of the United States]." We shall hereafter call this phrase the "jurisdiction requirement." Without that phrase, the clause would appear to demand a universal application, for it speaks of "*all*" persons, not some, and it employs a geographical referent (birth "in the United States") rather than a legal one. The jurisdiction requirement's conjunctive form, however, clearly suggests that it was meant to narrow the scope of the birthright citizenship principle under the clause. Indeed, we shall argue that the jurisdiction requirement should be understood to impose a consensual qualification on that principle.

The first clue to the meaning of the jurisdiction requirement can be found in its origins. As already noted, the phrase "and subject to the jurisdiction [of the United States]" displaced the earlier one in the 1866 act ("and not subject to any foreign power"), but the reason for this substitution remains obscure. Both formulations, however, were discussed during the debates over the act and the amendment, and by tracing Congress's evolving understanding of them, one can begin to discern the distinctive political conception that seemed to inspire both.

When the civil rights bill reached the Senate floor on January 29, 1866, it contained no citizenship provision. Senator Lyman Trumbull of Illinois, the chairman of the Committee on the Judiciary and the bill's floor manager, introduced an amendment to the bill declaring that "all persons of African descent born in the United States are hereby declared to be citizens of the United States."[12] This amendment obviously would have succeeded in overruling the *Dred Scott* decision, but it would have done so on the narrowest possible ground. The next day, before a vote was taken on his amendment, Trumbull moved to substitute another, broader amendment. It provided that "all persons born in the United States, and not subject to any foreign Power, are hereby declared to be citizens of the United States, without distinction of color."[13] He offered no explanation for this new proposal.

Immediately, the question was raised as to the provision's scope—in particular, whether Indians were meant to be included; Trumbull responded that he meant to include only those who were taxed, excluding all others. (The citizenship provision, as later enacted, contained such an exclusion).[14] Senator Edgar Cowan of Pennsylvania, a fierce opponent of the bill and an unregenerate racist, asked whether the citizenship provision would "have the effect of naturalizing the children of Chinese and Gypsies born in this country,"[15] to which Trumbull replied, "Undoubtedly."[16] A colloquy followed in which Trumbull strongly affirmed (and Cowan as strongly denied) that the American-born children of alien parents from China were already citizens under existing law.[17]

The Trumbull–Cowan exchange, especially when augmented by other references to the effect upon aliens of the citizenship provisions of the civil rights bill (and later, of the Fourteenth Amendment), clearly suggests that Congress understood itself to be extending birthright citizenship to the American-born children of Chinese and other resident aliens. It is all the more striking, then, that some thirty years later, when the Supreme Court first had occasion to consider the question directly in *United States* v. *Wong Kim Ark*,[18] the majority required more than fifty pages of argument to confirm that the Citizenship Clause had indeed extended birthright citizenship to an American-born son of permanent residents of California who happened to be Chinese subjects. The *Wong Kim Ark* majority's difficulty in reaching this conclusion probably reflected the troublesome fact that a treaty between China and the United States,[19] as well as the naturalization statute then in effect,[20] expressly disqualified Chinese parents and their children, as nonwhites, from becoming naturalized citizens. The dissenters, seizing upon this treaty provision, derided the suggestion that in the face of the Citizenship Clause's jurisdiction requirement, Wong Kim Ark's parents could obtain for him at birth the status of citizenship that the president and Congress, through treaty, statute, and the reciprocal action of the Chinese government with regard to American citizens, had so clearly meant to withhold from Chinese subjects.[21]

The legislative history of the Citizenship Clause, as we have seen, strongly supports the *Wong Kim Ark* majority's conclusion.[22] Congress *did* intend to extend birthright citizenship to individuals like Wong Kim Ark, whose parents were legal residents at the time of birth. It bears noting, however, that the debates also suggest that Congress probably extended it to such aliens with the expectation that its actual effect would be trivial. On several occasions during the debates, Congress was assured that the number of children of alien parents who would qualify for birthright citizenship under the clause would be *de minimis* and thus of no real concern.[23] This *de minimis* argument could not be credibly made with regard to the Indians, as several senators made clear.[24] This probably explains why, as we shall see, the debates were with a few exceptions preoccupied with the clause's effect upon them.[25]

These events—in particular, Congress's decision to move beyond the *Dred Scott* problem and the category of blacks to a more universal formulation ("all persons . . . not subject to any foreign Power") and its apparent recognition that the birthright citizenship provision would cover aliens' children—yielded a principle that would have profound significance for American society. By establishing beyond peradventure that the American-born children of resident aliens were (with exceptions discussed below) United States citizens by birth, and by subsequently enshrining that principle in the Citizenship Clause of the Fourteenth Amendment, the 39th Congress used ascription to give expansive shape to the American political community.

Expansive, but not universal. The jurisdiction requirement remained, marking an outer limit to the scope of the birthright citizenship principle. As the debate over the citizenship provision of the civil rights bill proceeded, some of its boundaries began to be explored. Senator Trumbull continued to be pressed, mostly in the context of objections to Indian citizenship, to articulate the boundaries of his citizenship proposal. Responding that his purpose was "to make citizens of everybody born in the United States who owe allegiance to the United States," Trumbull quickly noted the great difficulties in expressing the allegiance concept in statutory language (understandably so, since *all* Indians were held to owe *some* minimal allegiance). Alluding to the problem of diplomatic personnel who were domiciled in the United States temporarily, he observed that "we have no right to make citizens" of them or their children. Nevertheless, he added, they did (like Indians) owe the United States "a sort of allegiance," and thus a statute that sought to define citizenship in terms of allegiance "would not answer"; it would include groups meant to be excluded.[26]

This notion of allegiance—for Trumbull, the core concept of the "foreign power" exception—was refined somewhat as the Senate explicitly struggled to resolve the question of the citizenship status of Indians. Those debates revealed that Trumbull understood *allegiance* not chiefly in Coke's terms, as stemming from the fact of protection at birth, but in a more consensualist fashion, as dependent upon the wills of the community and the individual. As our earlier discussion suggests, the Indian question was an extremely sensitive one in view of the ambiguous legal status of the tribes, the varying degrees of assimilation of their members into white society, and racist feelings on the part of many white Americans.[27] Widespread agreement existed among the draftsmen of the 1866 act that birthright citizenship should extend only to certain Indians, presumably a small minority, who had in some (ill-defined) sense become assimilated into white society.[28] Several formulations were offered during the debates; each, however, was criticized as imprecise or under- or overinclusive. Senator Trumbull proposed to exclude "Indians not taxed," a phrase and category borrowed from the Apportionment Clause of the original Constitution.[29] There, Trumbull noted, the phrase had been used to designate "a class of persons who are not a part of our population [and] . . . are not regarded as a part of our people.[30]

Trumbull's amendment excluding "Indians not taxed" proved to be an acceptable compromise and became part of the 1866 act. But precisely because it was a compromise, it failed to elaborate clearly the more general principle that lay beneath the "foreign power" exception in the citizenship provision of the act. The contours of that principle and of the jurisdiction requirement to which it led, however, began to take more definite shape as Congress further considered the Indian question in the debates over the Fourteenth Amendment's Citizenship Clause only weeks later.

Immediately after Senator Jacob Howard introduced the clause as a change to Section 1 of the proposed Fourteenth Amendment, Senator James Doolittle of Wisconsin offered to amend Howard's amendment, which contained the jurisdiction requirement but did not refer to Indians, to exclude from the clause's coverage "Indians not taxed."[31] A lively debate ensued in which Doolittle argued that although "the Indians upon our reservations . . . are most clearly subject to our jurisdiction, both civil and military," they were never intended to be made citizens.[32] Senator Trumbull had wished to extend citizenship to all Indians living fully in white society, whether taxed or not, but had been obliged, as we have just seen, to accept a limitation in the 1866 act in order to assure its passage. Here, he maintained that "subject to the jurisdiction" of the United States meant subject to its "complete" jurisdiction; this meant "[n]ot owing allegiance to anybody else,"[33] an understanding that was consistent, as we have seen, with the earlier Indian cases and one that excluded all Indians with overriding tribal allegiances from United States citizenship.[34] Senator Reverdy Johnson of Maryland, however, interpreted "subject to the jurisdiction" in a far more inclusive fashion. For him, it was enough to justify citizenship for Indians that they were "within the territorial limits of the United States" and could be subjected to its criminal laws and other exercises of legislative authority.[35]

Senator Howard, the author of the Citizenship Clause, agreed with Trumbull that "jurisdiction" should be construed to mean "a full and complete jurisdiction," which he defined as "the same jurisdiction in extent and quality as applies to every citizen of the United States now." Accordingly, no Indians still "belonging to a tribal relation," with allegiances that were divided at best, could qualify under the clause. Hence, no special exclusionary language was necessary.[36] This view prevailed, fortified by the consideration that Section 2 of the Fourteenth Amendment would expressly exclude "Indians not taxed" from the population according to which Representatives were to be apportioned among the states.[37] The exclusionary language proposed by Doolittle was therefore rejected as superfluous.[38]

The debates over Indian citizenship did not merely resolve (at least for the time being) a nettlesome question of coverage under the Citizenship Clause, important as that resolution was. They also brought to the surface the central elements around which the 39th Congress organized its more general understanding of the scope and meaning of the jurisdiction requirement under the clause. In the clash between the rival conceptions of its scope that were articulated during the Senate debate, the more demanding formula-

tion—the idea of "full and complete jurisdiction," a jurisdiction precluding "allegiance to anybody else"—was the
one advanced by Senators Trumbull and Howard, the chief
architects of the clause and indeed of the Fourteenth
Amendment as a whole.[39]

Their view of the matter—that the existence of full and
reciprocal obligations of individual allegiance and governmental power and protection in this strong sense was the
crucial element needed to satisfy the jurisdiction requirement and qualify one for birthright citizenship under the
clause—echoed the consensualist public-law view as it had
been used by antebellum opponents of political equality for
Indians to defeat their ascriptive claims to citizenship at
birth. These people had successfully argued, as we have
seen, that because most Indians were members of separate,
even if dependent nations, they had never chosen or been
chosen to be United States citizens.[40] Hence they lacked full
allegiance to the United States government and had not been
granted its full reciprocal protection.

This view was subsequently reiterated by the Supreme
Court in 1884 when it decided the Indian citizenship case
Elk v. Wilkins.[41] In *Elk*, the Court majority held that the
Citizenship Clause did not confer birthright citizenship upon
an Indian who had been born into a tribe but had subsequently left it and resided in white society. Although born
in the United States, the Court held, consistently with
Worcester v. Georgia, that he was not born "subject to the
jurisdiction thereof." That phrase, the Court reasoned, required that the individual claiming birthright citizenship
be "not merely subject in some respect or degree to the

jurisdiction of the United States, but completely subject to their political jurisdiction, and owing them direct and immediate allegiance."[42]

The Court went on to unfold the ascriptive logic of birthright citizenship under the clause. In doing so, however, it also exposed the consensualist element that the jurisdiction requirement had introduced into the clause, one in tension with the older common-law view of the birthright principle. Speaking ascriptively, the court majority emphasized that under the clause, the jurisdiction requirement must be satisfied at "the time of birth" in order for birthright citizenship to attach—a requirement common to both the common-law and public-law positions.[43] At the same time, the Court explicitly read the clause's jurisdiction requirement as a repository of consensual ideas. The jurisdiction requirement demanded *reciprocal* consent—not only the complete allegiance of the individual (which might be actual or, as in the case of children, ascribed), but also the consent of the nation to his membership. To the Court, the jurisdiction requirement exemplified "the principle that no one can become a citizen of a nation without its consent."[44] That requirement, the Court observed, was inconsistent with the "theory that Indians do or can make themselves independent citizens" by any unilateral act on their part such as joining white society; the government, and not just the individual, must explicitly consent to full membership.[45] The Citizenship Clause had not altered the principle, evident in Marshall's decisions in the early Indian cases and grounded in the Vattelian view of political membership, that the individual's consent alone did not suffice.

Although the meaning of the jurisdiction requirement

was elaborated most fully and carefully in connection with the congressional debates (and later adjudication) over the question of Indian birthright citizenship, it was further confirmed by Congress in the context of its discussions of another, less controversial implication of the requirement: the exclusion from birthright citizenship of American-born children of foreign diplomats. This result, of course, was never in doubt. The debates over both the 1866 act and the Fourteenth Amendment disclose no dissent from the view that diplomats and their children were not "subject to the jurisdiction" of the United States for purposes of the clause. This reflected the extraterritorial immunity from domestic law enjoyed by diplomats, an immunity that in turn reflects certain special factors, including the ancient rule affirming the personal inviolability of ambassadors, the imperatives of diplomatic secrecy, and reciprocity between nations.[46] But it was also fully consistent with the meaning of the jurisdiction requirement that has been developed here. Thus, diplomatic families, owing allegiance to their home countries, bore an attachment to the United States and a subjection to its laws even less extensive than that borne by Indians, who were chiefly attached to dependent tribes. Moreover, this privileged status of diplomats was one to which both governments consented, one indeed that was vital to their sovereign interests.

The jurisdiction requirement, then, can best be understood as having added to the ineradicably ascriptive birthright citizenship rule a transforming consensual conception of the necessary connection between an individual and his government—a conception that was, in the manner of Burlamaqui and Vattel, more profoundly *political* than one emphasizing the individual's mere presence on the soil at birth.[47] The connection must be more than simply the individual's subjection to the government's police power and criminal jurisdiction, more even than the individuals's manifest desire for membership in the political community and the absence of any similar allegiance (in Senator Trumbull's words) "to anyone else."[48] It also demanded a more or less complete, direct power by government over the individual, and a reciprocal relationship between them at the time of birth, in which the government consented to the individual's presence and status and offered him complete protection. In the public-law view, as we have seen, this protection and citizenship extended to the child, but only through the government's consent to the parents, whose consent was in turn taken provisionally to stand for that of the child.[49] In this way, even birthright citizenship's inherently ascriptive nature flowed from consensualist commitments.

This more consensualist reading of the Citizenship Clause is supported by the fact that, although it imposed an obligation of allegiance upon the native-born citizen, Congress could not have conceived of that obligation as perpetual or indissoluble on his part. Only one day before the Fourteenth Amendment was ratified, Congress embraced the consensual conception of citizenship in a more direct and thoroughgoing way, affirming in the Expatriation Act of 1868 the fundamental right of all citizens voluntarily to withdraw their consent and to renounce their citizenship.[50] That act clearly established the principle that membership in the political community must always reflect the individual citizen's consent, a consent that must remain vital and continuing lest the individual withdraw it.

Furthermore, this unequivocal right of self-expatriation was eventually understood to have created a fundamental assymmetry in the nature of American citizenship, one in which an individual citizen could *always* sever the political relationship by withdrawing his consent at any time, but the government could *never* do so.[51] If the consent required to create that relationship was a two-way street traveled largely by the government, as in the cases of *Dred Scott* and *Elk*, dissolution of that relationship through expatriation would eventually be a one-way street reserved for the exclusive use of the individual. That asymmetry stems from the nation's commitment to the belief that its consensual authority should be exercised in ways that secure fundamental human rights. Any recognition of a governmental power to denationalize citizens came to be seen, quite reasonably, as an abrogation of the government's obligation to protect the individual's rights too great to be sustained. In a polity grounded on the principle of consent but committed to fair, humanitarian policies, this unilateral power to expatriate oneself has made a rule of ascriptive birthright citizenship seem a generous, acceptable pragmatic solution to a knotty theoretical and practical problem.

The 1868 Expatriation Act did not, however, lay out any procedures by which expatriation could occur; it was more concerned to assert the right and then guarantee the protection of the United States for all those who wished to exercise that right and become Americans. While the act was subsequently interpreted to provide an expatriation right to native-born Americans as well, its value as a move toward more consensually based citizenship was largely symbolic. It was left to the executive branch, chiefly the State Department, to define appropriate procedures for expatriation, although Congress did eventually codify the practices that emerged in a new expatriation statute in 1907.[52] Those procedures have been modified since, but they ordinarily require residence overseas for expatriation to be acknowledged by the United States; expatriation within the country is provided for only during war, and only with the attorney general's confirmation that the renunciation is not "contrary to the interests of national defense."[53] Removal from the country is, of course, frequently a decisive obstacle to any desire to seek expatriation. Hence the law's failure fully to realize a consensualist commitment to a practical right of expatriation has never been wholly remedied.

At any rate, the joinder of birthright citizenship to a general right of expatriation is more a marriage of convenience than a wholly satisfying union. It is problematic, first, because it does not answer all of the legitimate objections to ascriptive membership at birth raised by the consensual view. For example, a native-born child may subsequently be required to risk his life in military service, perhaps on behalf of a cause he never embraced, in return for benefits he never chose. Because the only recognized procedures for expatriation usually involve physical removal from the country, the existing right of expatriation does not practically resolve this problem.

Moreover, most countries, including the United States, claim the power to forestall expatriation during national emergencies, just at the time when the birthright citizen feels most burdened by his ascribed obligations.[54] The debate over military service in the Vietnam era showed how unconvincing the ascription of "tacit consent" could appear to individuals compelled because of their place of birth to fight against their will.[55] If such obligations are to be legitimated in a principled fashion, the tension between birthright citizenship and the consensual principle must be confronted.

Furthermore, America's current circumstances confirm that birthright citizenship can create a problem of overinclusiveness, at least in consensual terms. In particular, automatic political membership for the native-born children of illegal aliens and nonimmigrants seems difficult to defend, especially when access to citizenship for other needy groups must be limited. These questions are analyzed in chapter 4. That analysis, we think, indicates the desirability of modifying the current law of birthright citizenship in favor of a more consensual view, a reform that we detail in chapter 5.

4   BIRTHRIGHT CITIZENSHIP IN THE CONTEMPORARY POLITY

We have argued that birthright citizenship's historical and philosophical origins make it strikingly anomalous as a key constitutive element of a liberal political system. This position naturally raises the question of why birthright citizenship has not only survived into the modern era but has flourished during a period in which other ascriptive legal statuses have been utterly discredited and in which consent has become the most important, durable legitimating principle in American political life.

It is tempting to explain the birthright citizenship rule as nothing more than a vestigial remnant, the kind of legal survival that a rationalizing law has not yet gotten around to discarding.[1] Such an explanation, however, ignores the very real advantages that a birthright citizenship rule still possesses. Some of these advantages simply reflect those of ascription generally, which were discussed in chapter 1; others relate to the distinctive context of American history. To begin with, birthright citizenship is by now familiar, having long been the rule of the common law, canonized as such by Blackstone.[2] It also remains a legal rule that is manifestly easy to apply. Perhaps most important, the inclusiveness of the birthright citizenship rule, which must have seemed especially attractive to the liberal framers of the Fourteenth Amendment who ardently wished to renounce the legacy of *Dred Scott*, has the effect today of removing a legal disability that would otherwise afflict many children of illegal aliens. Many Americans may favor this outcome on humanitarian grounds. It is perhaps not surprising, then, that so well-established, easily applied, and inclusive a rule would commend itself to courts and constitution-makers alike. To a pragmatic political system, the fact that birthright citizenship derived historically from alien philosophical premises may in the end have seemed less important than the fact that it has "worked" in the sense of performing practical tasks that have been set for it. Here, as elsewhere, the "If it ain't broke, don't fix it" principle may have seemed decisive.

Two recent and somewhat related developments, however, have begun to place far greater strain on this ideological compromise. The massive increase in illegal migration to the United States and the equally dramatic rise of the welfare state have transformed perhaps the greatest advantage of birthright citizenship from a modern liberal viewpoint—its automatic inclusiveness—into something of a disadvantage. By underscoring the growing practical importance of consent as the chief constitutive political principle of a liberal society, these developments invite us to reconsider on legal and policy grounds a practice that we have also found to be ideologically anomalous. This reconsideration occupies the next two sections. It leads us to reject the traditional rule and to propose, in the final chapter, a more consensualist law of citizenship in which ascribed status at birth plays a correspondingly reduced role.

The Problem of Illegal Migration

When the framers of the Citizenship Clause adopted (in a significantly compromised form) the common-law rule of birthright citizenship, immigration to the United States was entirely unregulated. The nation maintained a policy of completely open borders for almost another decade, when the first exclusion law, barring prostitutes and vagabonds, was enacted.[3] Indeed, until well into the first decade of this century, birthright citizenship could plausibly be understood as one ingredient of an integrated national strategy to encourage immigration in order to populate a vast, essentially empty continent with the need for more laborers, mechanics, and farmers than American society itself could produce.[4] An open-border policy was also celebrated as a way to serve liberal, humanitarian values, to make America an "asylum" for the "oppresssed and persecuted of all Nations and Religions," as George Washington had urged at the outset.[5]

Today, of course, that strategy of open borders is a distant memory, bearing about as much relationship to current immigration policy concerns as the horse-and-buggy does to contemporary modes of transportation. Beginning in the last quarter of the nineteenth century, the consensual principle, which had earlier been applied to exclude Indians and blacks from membership, was used even more restrictively.

Systematic efforts to stem the tide of immigration began with the Chinese exclusion acts of the 1880s and 1890s[6] and were continued in the so-called Gentlemen's Agreement excluding Japanese,[7] in racial restrictions on eligibility for naturalization,[8] and in the ethnocentric national origins quota system.[9] When Congress largely abandoned this system in 1965, it substituted another set of national and hemispheric quotas—more even-handed and benign, to be sure, but only slightly less restrictive.[10] After the Bracero program ended in 1964, legal entry of Mexicans was severely reduced. Illegal migration from Mexico increased dramatically thereafter, especially during the 1970s and 1980s, when that flow was swollen by illegal migration from the Caribbean Basin and Central America, and by large refugee movements from Southeast Asia. Political convulsions elsewhere, such as the Iranian revolution and martial law in Poland, encouraged numerous students, tourists, and other "nonimmigrant" visitors to remain here in violation of their visa restrictions.

The number of illegal aliens presently in the United States is a matter of great and continuing controversy; estimates that are described as "conservative" place the range at three and a half to six million as of 1980, with the number increasing by two hundred thousand annually.[11] This reality and the fears that it has generated concerning its economic and social effects have transformed political discourse about American immigration policy in ways that neither the ascriptive-minded court in *Lynch* v. *Clarke* nor the Reconstruction framers of the Citizenship Clause could have anticipated. "Control of our borders," not encouragement of immigration, now dominates contemporary policy discussions.[12] This slogan symbolizes a more profound, normative debate concerning the future of American pluralism and the appropriate size, shape, and composition of the polity.[13] This debate has been renewed periodically during this century but never decisively resolved. It has occurred most recently around the Simpson-Mazzoli legislation, which was narrowly defeated at the end of the 98th Congress.[14] The illegal alien phenomenon, however, has placed this continuing debate in a context in which different political values and trade-offs have become salient. Viewed in this light, the eternal questions surrounding citizenship—how and by whom it is to be acquired, and what rights and duties it is to imply—assume a rather different aspect than they have in earlier national debates.

If mutual consent is the irreducible condition of membership in the American polity, it is difficult to defend a practice that extends birthright citizenship to the native-born children of illegal aliens. The parents of such children are, by definition, individuals whose presence within the jurisdiction of the United States is prohibited by law. They are manifestly individuals, therefore, to whom the society has explicitly and self-consciously decided to deny membership. And if the society has refused to consent to their membership, it can hardly be said to have consented to that of their children who happen to be born while their parents are here in clear violation of American law.

As we discuss below,[15] the present guarantee under American law of automatic birthright citizenship to the children of illegal aliens can only operate, at the margin, as one more incentive to illegal migration and violation by nonimmigrant (temporary visitor) aliens already here of their time-limited visa restrictions. When this attraction is combined with the powerful lure of the expanded entitlements conferred upon citizen children and their families by the modern welfare state, the total incentive effect of birthright citizenship may well become significant. Certainly, it cannot be ignored. Needless to say, attempts to estimate the precise magnitude of this effect—the number of birthright citizens born to illegal alien parents who would not otherwise have come here—face insuperable data limitations. In addition to anecdotal evidence that many aliens do cross the border illegally to assure United States citizenship for their soon-to-be-born children,[16] a very recent study illuminates two features of this phenomenon. First, the number of births in the United States to illegal alien parents is not trivial; a conservative estimate places the number as in excess of seventy-five thousand each year.[17] Second, these births—and the public costs that they entail—seem to be disproportionately concentrated in a relatively few urban areas.[18]

Congress is not impotent in the face of this challenge to consensualism. Although the Citizenship Clause of the Fourteenth Amendment has been assumed to guarantee birthright citizenship to such children *ex proprio vigore*,[19] the evidence that we reviewed in chapter 3 suggests a rather different conclusion. First, the debates that preceded Congress's adoption of the clause establish that the 39th Congress neither considered, nor could have been expected to consider, this question. It legislated in a world in which unrestricted immigration to the United States was actually encouraged. The question of the citizenship status of the native-born children of illegal aliens never arose for the simple reason that no illegal aliens existed at that time, or indeed for some time thereafter.[20]

Second, the debates also establish that the framers of the Citizenship Clause had no intention of establishing a universal rule of birthright citizenship. To be sure, they intended to do more than simply extend citizenship to native-born blacks by overruling the reasoning and result in *Dred Scott*. But they also intended, through the clause's jurisdiction requirement, to limit the scope of birthright citizenship. The essential limiting principle, discernible from the debates (especially those concerned with the citizenship status of Indians) was consensualist in nature. Citizenship, as qualified by this principle, was not satisfied by mere birth on the soil or by naked governmental power or legal jurisdiction over the individual. Citizenship required in addition the existence of conditions indicating mutual consent to political membership.[21]

It would be wrong to suggest that either the content or the measure of this principle, most particularly its requirement of mutual consent, was well specified in the debates. Nor would its application to particular individuals or groups always yield clear and uncontroversial citizenship determinations under the clause. Moreover, as we discuss below, even if applying the consent principle on a case-by-case basis were not difficult, it would surely be dangerous. For that reason we firmly oppose using it in that way.[22] Our argument, however, does not require that the consent principle be applied case-by-case. It is enough to say that whatever the proper reach of the consent principle may be, it cannot logically be applied to include the native-born children of illegal aliens, to whom the nation's consent has expressly been denied.

An illuminating perspective on this point is provided by

the dissenting opinion in *Elk v. Wilkins*, the Indian citizenship case discussed earlier.[23] There, Justice John M. Harlan argued eloquently that the plaintiff, who had come to reside in white society with the consent of the state, satisfied the jurisdiction requirement and therefore came within the ambit of the Citizenship Clause. To deny him birthright citizenship, Harlan argued, would pervert the spirit of the clause by maintaining in the United States "a despised and rejected class of persons, with no nationality whatever; who, born in our territory, owing no allegiance to any foreign power, and subject, as residents of the States, to all the burdens of government, are not yet members of any political community nor entitled to any of the rights, privileges, or immunities of citizens of the United States."[24]

This argument suggests that even those, like Harlan, who viewed birthright citizenship under the clause most expansively, still defined its purposes in terms that would, if applied in today's context, exclude illegal aliens. Illegal aliens, in Harlan's terms, are less needful of birthright citizenship than even the plaintiff in *Elk*. They almost always possess another nationality, owe allegiance to a foreign power, and are therefore members of a political community, whether or not they choose to return and take up that membership. If the native-born, adult Indian who lived openly in American society but who had none of these protections (except, perhaps, from a "domestic, dependent nation") did not enjoy birthright citizenship under the clause, then it is difficult to understand why the native-born child of illegal aliens, who ordinarily retains all such protections, should be constitutionally preferred.

Several distinctions are in order. We are not arguing that

such children are not entitled to any legal protection. Indeed, we emphatically acknowledge the possibility that those children (and perhaps their parents as well) may have legitimate moral or humanitarian claims upon American society. Those claims might arise in several different ways. For example, we may be said to have incurred moral obligations to illegal aliens by encouraging them to migrate here, by enriching ourselves through their labor, by absorbing them into our communities, by inviting legitimate expectations of humane treatment, and perhaps by other behavior.[25] We do not propose to explore here whether in fact the United States has incurred such moral obligations and, if so, what the nature and extent of those obligations might be. For present purposes, our point is that even if moral obligations to illegal aliens exist and are compelling, they by no means imply a moral claim—and certainly not a birthright entitlement—to American citizenship.

Again, that does not mean that policy toward illegal aliens is morally unconstrained. For children who have already been born here of illegal alien parents, for example, a retroactive change in the law depriving them of their citizenship status would violate important expectation and reliance interests and create great confusion and uncertainty. As noted previously, those who have grown up within the United States, considering themselves citizens and planning accordingly, are in fact organically part of and dependent upon the American community for fulfillment of many of their most basic needs and aspirations.[26] Changing their status thus could quite plausibly be seen as a failure by the state to fulfill its liberal obligations to respect fundamental rights of these persons. For these reasons, we would maintain birthright citizenship for all individuals who, prior to the effective date of our proposed change, were born under the existing interpretation of the Citizenship Clause. In addition, it may well prove to be desirable as a matter of legislative policy to grant legal status, including eventual access to citizenship by naturalization, to illegal aliens and their families who have resided here for substantial periods of time and have forged significant ties to the American community. In principle, we strongly favor such an "amnesty" for long-term resident illegal aliens and their families, while recognizing the difficulties inherent in any limited amnesty plan and the importance of the programmatic details in any evaluation of the prospects for successfully implementing it.

But these concessions to prudence, fairness, and liberal humanitarianism should not be taken to deny to the American community the essence of a consensual political identity—the power and obligation to seek to define its own boundaries and enforce them. If Congress should conclude that the prospective denial of birthright citizenship to the children of illegal aliens would be a valuable adjunct of such national self-definition, the Constitution should not be interpreted in a way that impedes that effort. Illegal aliens, however admirable their initiative in seeking to come here, seem poorly situated, morally speaking, to contest that policy choice. They have migrated here, after all, in knowing defiance of American law, well aware that they may at any moment be obliged to return. If anybody may be said to have taken a calculated risk, they can. Moreover, almost all deported illegal aliens return to their own countries, of which they are still members. Although they would rather not do so—or would prefer to do so at a time of their own choosing—such preferences taken alone are ordinarily not morally compelling. Finally, citizenship status is not necessary to afford illegal aliens and their children at least minimal legal protection and public benefits, for they possess certain procedural and substantive rights under the Constitution merely by reason of their presence within the United States.[27] We do not take any position here concerning what the precise nature and extent of those rights ought to be. It is enough for present purposes to affirm that the Constitution need not and should not be woodenly interpreted either to guarantee their children citizenship or to cast them into outer darkness.

A more difficult question arises if an illegal alien parent or child should, under our proposal, be rendered stateless or have no citizenship to which they could safely return. (Most nations, including Mexico, *do* regard children born abroad to their nationals as their citizens.) If a "well-founded fear of persecution" in their home country should prevent them from returning there, political asylum might be available.[28] If not, other forms of administrative relief—"extended voluntary departure,"[29] suspension of deportation,[30] "deferred action status,"[31] withholding of deportation,[32] and others—could be granted. Moreover, as we note below, evolving international law norms antagonistic to statelessness may in extreme cases impute a nationality, although not citizenship, to an otherwise stateless individual. Finally, as a matter of policy, we favor enlarged refugee quotas and more liberal treatment of asylum seekers with nonfrivolous claims of persecution.

But the possibility of relief of these kinds is a separate

issue, logically unconnected to the question of whether birthright American citizenship for illegal alien children is or ought to be mandated by the Constitution. As Vattel emphasized long ago, humanitarian claims set moral standards for a nation's use of its powers of self-determination, but recognition of the rights of its existing citizens means that such claims cannot obviate those powers.

The question of whether the Constitution guarantees birthright citizenship to the native-born children of illegal aliens is also analytically separate from the question of how inclusive or restrictive American immigration policy in general ought to be. But if, as we maintain, no constitutional mandate of birthright citizenship for such children exists, then the question of their status would become an important issue that Congress would have to resolve as a policy matter, weighing their claims for admission against those of other groups—such as overseas refugees, asylum-seekers, visa applicants, and family members—with different but plausible claims. As we discuss below, the authors strongly favor a policy concerning admission of refugees and legal aliens for permanent residence that would be far more generous than current law permits.[33] We further believe, although we cannot demonstrate, that more effective controls over the influx of illegal aliens, of which denial of birthright citizenship to their native-born children is one small part, might well reduce somewhat the opposition to a more generous admissions policy. For present purposes, the important point is that there is no logical, ideological, or perhaps even political inconsistency between a policy that increases legal immigration levels and one that eliminates birthright citizenship for illegal alien children. Instead, these measures can work harmoniously as part of a broader program to reduce the number of illegal aliens.

It should be noted that all of the arguments that we have made against birthright citizenship for the children of illegal aliens apply with equal or greater force to the children of so-called nonimmigrants, aliens who have been allowed to enter under visa restrictions only for a limited period of time and for limited purposes.[34] Unlike the situation with citizens and legal resident aliens, the government has declined to consent to their political membership or permanent presence in the society; indeed, it has admitted them on the express condition that they confine their activities and leave within a specified period. On the view of the Citizenship Clause that we have advanced, their children born here should not be regarded as having been born "subject to the jurisdiction" of the United States. The number of nonimmigrants is considerably larger than the number of illegal aliens; in 1983, there were almost ten million nonimmigrant admissions.[35] Unfortunately, reliable estimates of the number of native-born children of nonimmigrants are not available.[36]

If the Citizenship Clause, with its consent-based jurisdiction requirement, was never intended to extend birthright citizenship to the native-born children of today's flood of illegal and nonimmigrant aliens, the Supreme Court's recent endorsement of the traditional view seems especially problematic. In *Plyler* v. *Doe*, the Court suggested that the Citizenship Clause, by using the word *jurisdiction* in a "predominantly geographic sense," constituted the native-born children of illegal aliens as birthright citizens.[37] It must be said in criticism that the Court's treatment of the question was notably casual; it was relegated to *dictum* in a footnote that took the form of a deeply flawed syllogism. The major premise of this syllogism—that the *Wong Kim Ark* case[38] had decided the birthright citizenship issue as to illegal alien children—is, as we have seen, simply incorrect.[39] Its minor premise—that *jurisdiction* must mean precisely the same thing in both the Citizenship and Equal Protection Clauses of Section I—is at least questionable.[40] Its conclusion—that the Equal Protection Clause protects illegal aliens—is correct but has no direct bearing on the question of their citizenship.[41] The only other support that the Court offered for its position was a 1912 treatise that simply parroted the common-law view and read it, by way of *Wong Kim Ark*, into the clause.[42] In short, the Court did not carefully consider and reject the political, consensualist understanding of the jurisdiction requirement, and hence of the clause, that we have advanced. Rather, it ignored that view in its haste to comment upon an issue that was not, and has not been, squarely before it. As the next section suggests, the Court's position is not simply unconvincing and reflexive constitutional exegesis; it also constitutes questionable public policy.

The Emergence of the Welfare State

The ethos of the modern welfare state traces its beginnings to the New Deal, but it has emerged full-blown only during the last two decades.[43] Although the appropriate size and shape of the welfare state are still very much matters

of intense public debate, its permanence seems assured.
Even the Reagan Administration, surely the most conservative since the 1920s, has been obliged to pay reluctant
obeisance to the essential elements of the new social order.
Far from removing the so-called safety net programs, Reagan has managed only to slow their rate of expansion and
to enlarge some of the openings in the net's mesh.[44] Even
a national consensus on the need to reduce massive budget
deficits reveals little evidence of a social disposition to dis-
mantle its basic structure.

Of the many social changes wrought by the welfare state,
surely two of the least discussed have been its effects upon
the role and significance of citizenship[45] and upon the incentives for illegal immigration. Those effects, however, are
related and, taken together, appear to have been considerable. By altering the role of government and individuals
and by transforming their relationships with one another,
the welfare state has raised important new questions about
the nature of citizenship. And by changing the stakes in
immigration, the welfare state has also placed the question
of birthright citizenship for the children of illegal aliens in
a new light.

Until the 1930s, the federal government largely confined
itself to producing public goods and enforcing common-
law property rights on behalf of individuals. In such a world,
American citizenship was a status that carried few affirmative obligations other than military service and taxation,
and only the rights, mostly "negative" ones, that traditional
liberal government conferred: the right to vote,[46] to own
property, to avoid deportation, and to resist governmental
intrusions upon constitutionally protected interests.

The New Deal changed all that. Three developments seem

especially significant for understanding the contemporary meaning of citizenship. First, in the post–New Deal years, especially during the 1960s and 1970s, the federal government (and to a lesser extent, the states) became the creator and guarantor of what Charles Reich has called "new property" rights.[47] These included an array of valuable legal statuses and entitlements enforceable by individuals and groups against public resources. Twenty years ago, well before their full efflorescence, Reich tried to convey the bewildering variety of these new rights and their implications for political relationships:[48]

One of the most important developments in the United States during the past decade has been the emergence of government as a major source of wealth. Government is a gigantic syphon. It draws in revenue and power, and pours forth wealth: money, benefits, services, contracts, franchises, and licenses. Government has always had this function. But while in early times it was minor, today's distribution of largess is on a vast, imperial scale.

The valuables dispensed by government take many forms, but they all share one characteristic. They are steadily taking the place of traditional forms of wealth— forms which are held as private property. Social insurance substitutes for savings; a government contract replaces a businessman's customers and goodwill. The wealth of more and more Americans depends upon a relationship to government. Increasingly, Americans live on government largess—allocated by government on its own terms, and held by recipient subject to conditions which express "the public interest."

The growth of government largess, accompanied by

a distinctive system of law, is having profound consequences. It affects the underpinnings of individualism and independence. It influences the workings of the Bill of Rights. It has an impact on the power of private interests, in their relation to each other and to government. It is helping to create a new society.

This far-reaching development has been accompanied, facilitated, and legitimated by another set of even more fundamental changes in the legal order. Although these changes, which Schuck has elsewhere characterized as "communitarian" in nature,[49] have occurred in disparate areas of public and private law, they reveal some common themes. Thus, the law has increasingly expanded the scope of individual and governmental liability, locating the sources of enlarged obligation not only in consent and traditional tort principles, but in expansive notions of social policy and morality. The law also increasingly speaks of individuals' "rights," the language of entitlement, rather than of their "interests," the language of policy and accommodation. Moreover, the law increasingly emphasizes the values of equality, group interest, and nondiscrimination. Through these new norms and techniques, the legal order has generally strengthened the procedural and substantive claims of individuals against government (and private powerholders).[50]

While the welfare state was enlarging the scope of government's obligations to individuals, the status of citizenship was undergoing several important changes that reflected the past evolution of the welfare state and would influence its future shape. First, Congress reduced the symbolic value of citizenship by eliminating the universal duty of military service except in time of emergency,[51] one of the few duties of citizenship in a liberal state. Whatever its merits, this policy diluted a preeminent feature of political membership—the sense of shared sacrifice and patriotic commitment to a common goal.[52]

Second, a line of judicial decisions significantly lowered the political and economic value of citizenship by prohibiting government, especially the states, from allocating certain legal rights and economic advantages on the basis of that status.[53] In the most important of these decisions, *Graham* vs. *Richardson*,[54] the Supreme Court invalidated statutes that restricted welfare benefits to United States citizens and legal resident aliens who had resided in the United States for fifteen years. The Court held that alienage was a constitutionally "suspect classification," one that could not ordinarily be used as a basis for allocating state-created advantages between citizens and aliens.

The current status of *Graham* is much discussed in the cases and legal commentary.[55] Generally speaking, its principle has been extended to invalidate citizenship requirements for some, but not all, professions and occupations regulated by state law.[56] It has been held inapplicable to citizenship requirements for federally created entitlements, such as Medicare,[57] and for federal civil service jobs.[58] Even as qualified and limited by later cases, however, *Graham's* repudiation of citizenship as a criterion for allocating the welfare state's "new property" entitlements is significant. Both in its radical departure from earlier case law on the validity of alienage classifications and in its refusal to regard citizenship as a special status entitling its holder to special advantages in the welfare state, *Graham* marks an important milestone in the devaluation of citizenship.

These three developments, then—the creation of "new

property" rights, the embedding of these rights in a legal order more congenial to the assertion of individual claims against government, and the declining importance of citizenship as a distinctive political and legal status to which special rights and obligations attach—have fundamentally altered the meaning of American citizenship. But these changes have also had another far-reaching effect. By vastly increasing the resources that government allocates, the welfare state has significantly raised the stakes in obtaining the legal status that assures access to those resources. That status, however, is no longer citizenship; indeed, after *Plyler*, it is no longer even legal residence. *Graham* and its progeny have defined membership in the welfare state far more broadly than political membership.

And it is welfare state membership, not citizenship, that increasingly counts.[59] Political membership uniquely confers little more than the right to vote and the right to remain here permanently; the former is used at most by only a bare majority of eligible voters,[60] while the latter, although undeniably valuable, is problematic for only a minority of legal aliens.[61] Membership in the welfare state, in contrast, is of crucial and growing significance; for some, who are wholly dependent upon public benefits, it may literally be a matter of life or death.

This shift in the salience of memberships has subtly affected the role of consent in legitimating the government's activities. As to welfare state membership, the individual's actual consent is virtually automatic and to that extent meaningless. The price for joining, after all, is almost zero, while the advantages have never been greater and in some cases may overwhelm all other considerations. The government's consent to individuals' membership in the welfare state is also virtually automatic and thus meaningless, but for a different reason. A more communitarian judiciary increasingly compels government to consent by imposing obligations toward aliens that it has not voluntarily undertaken; sometimes, as in *Graham*, courts override the legislature's explicit refusal to consent.[62]

But if the centrality of American citizenship has declined for those already here legally, it remains valuable nonetheless, especially for those who seek to escape the turbulent social conditions that often prevail today outside our borders. American citizenship not only assures one access to the fruits of the welfare state but to a permanent freedom from the persecution, economic disaster, or chronic instability that are the lot of most individuals in the world. For many of these aliens, the prospect of conferring birthright American citizenship upon their soon-to-be-born children surely influences their decisions to come or remain here illegally.

Consider the consequences of successfully obtaining that status, both for the native-born child and for the illegal alien parents. For the child, American citizenship will mean the ability to come and remain here whenever and for as long as he likes, to participate in public life, to work in the American economy without blatant exploitation, and to claim the full protection of American law, including all of the benefits of the welfare state. Viewed purely in economic terms—surely a revealing, albeit inadequate, measure of the value of guaranteed citizenship at birth—these advantages are enormous. The magnitude involved is suggested by comparing the lifetime income stream of a child born in 1982 in Mexico who lives his life there, and his counterpart born and living in the United States. The expected life income of the former is less than $150,000; that of the latter is almost $1 million—a difference of over 650 percent.[63]

We do not wish to suggest that Mexican parents know these data in any precise sense. We maintain only that it is plausible to believe that differential life opportunities of this order of magnitude do not go unnoticed and are highly relevant to their decision concerning whether and when to migrate illegally across the highly porous southern border. Except in the (presumably rare) case of parents who derive no personal benefits from knowing that their child's life chances would increase so dramatically simply by being born in the United States, one would expect that parental love would fuel a strong desire to assure an American birth for their child, at least in those for whom migration costs are not very high. But even if we assume that the parents are selfish—even if they derive no personal value from vastly increasing their child's life chances—birthright citizenship for the child would be extremely advantageous to the parents.

First, illegal aliens with citizen children are somewhat less likely to be deported than if their children are aliens. Under current law, illegal alien parents who are apprehended by the immigration authorities are subject to deportation despite the fact that one or more of their children is a United States citizen and therefore is legally entitled to remain here.[64] Parents in such situations may apply to an immigration judge (and, if unsuccessful, to an administrative court and then to the federal courts) for relief from deportation on the ground that either of the family's alternatives—leaving the citizen children here while the rest of the family (parents and noncitizen children) return to their own country, or departing as a family, thereby depriving the citizen children of their American birthright—constitutes an "extreme hardship" for which suspension of deportation is warranted under the law.[65] Even when such claims are rejected, as they often are,[66] they tend to delay the deportation proceedings, especially when this "extreme hardship" claim is bolstered by other mitigating or extenuating factors ("equities," in the jargon of immigration practice) such as the pendency of an asylum application, close family ties to a legal permanent resident or adult citizen, and the like. Even for the alien who will ultimately be deported, such delays are likely to be extremely valuable.[67]

Second, the parents may eventually be able to "bootstrap" their child's citizen status into legal residence (and eventually citizenship) for the parents themselves. Once the child reaches majority, he may file a petition for legal permanent residence status on behalf of the parents. This petition would be routinely granted and the parents immediately admitted as legal permanent residents, without regard to quota limitations.[68]

Third, the parents may obtain welfare and other public benefits for their citizen children, if not directly for themselves; even the former will relieve the parents of substantial financial burdens. Very recently, for example, the California Supreme Court struck down state AFDC (Aid to Families with Dependent Children) regulations that required the state to exclude consideration of the needs of an illegal alien mother and her illegal alien children from the computation of AFDC eligibility and benefit levels available to the several citizen children in the family. The court held that the exclusion of the illegal alien mother and children's needs effectively reduced the benefit level received by their citizen siblings through no fault of the latter, and that this reduction therefore violated their constitutional rights.[69]

The principle of this case—that illegal alien parents and siblings can piggy-back benefits from the existence in their household of birthright citizen children—is important, for the phenomenon of mixed-status households is exceedingly common. A recent study of undocumented aliens in Texas, for example, found that about half of the households in which undocumented aliens lived contained United States–born citizens as well as illegal aliens.[70] Nonimmigrant aliens, whose native-born children would, under current practice, also automatically receive birthright citizenship, also have access to benefits on similar terms.

Nobody, of course, can accurately calculate the full costs and the offsetting social benefits associated with the rule of birthright citizenship as a lure to illegal and nonimmigrant alien parents. Part of the difficulty relates to our ignorance about the extent to which the availability of birthright citizenship increases the level of illegal migration that would otherwise exist. Obviously, other incentives to migrate illegally are already very great. Still, the prospect of one's children obtaining birthright citizenship presumably increases those incentives at the margin.[71]

In any event, birthright citizen children of illegal and nonimmigrant aliens clearly require significant expenditures of public resources. Public hospitals, for example, report that a substantial majority of their maternity admissions are illegal aliens who are about to give birth to citizen children, and the available data support this claim.[72] The unpaid maternity bills for illegal aliens in only three public hospitals in Los Angeles County alone cost those hospitals, and thus taxpayers, an estimated $20.1 million in 1983.[73] And maternity care, of course, is only one of the public services involved.[74]

To some degree, illegal aliens defray the costs of public benefits and services through their tax payments. The magnitude of this compensating effect is a complex question; the data are poor, each tax is financed and structured differently, and the actual incidence of certain taxes is unclear. Very recent studies in Texas and California present somewhat conflicting conclusions in this regard.[75] Another difficulty relates to the much-disputed effects of illegal migration on unemployment and wage levels and thus on the unemployment benefits and other unemployment-related services for American citizens and legal aliens.[76] Yet another relates to possible longer-term changes in the pattern of benefits to illegal aliens, such as those that may result from their reaching old age in the United States.[77]

In the end, the question of birthright citizenship for the children of illegal and nonimmigrant aliens probably should not turn on the conclusions that such revenue-cost analyses reach, important as those analyses may be for policy guidance. Instead, we believe, this question should be resolved in the light of broader ideals of constitutional meaning, social morality, and political community. These ideals militate against constitutionally ascribed birthright citizenship in these circumstances. As the earlier discussion suggests, the Citizenship Clause was never intended to guarantee citizenship for such individuals. Beyond the question of textual analysis, moreover, it is simply morally perverse to reward law-breaking by conferring the valued status of citizenship, and it is even more perverse to plant that guarantee in the Constitution. It is true that illegal entry ordinarily is a mere misdemeanor[78] and that the lawbreakers are often individuals whose ambition, resourcefulness, and family values most Americans would admire.[79] Nevertheless, the objection remains a powerful one.

Another normative argument against birthright citizenship for such individuals relates to the relative weakness of their moral claims. The crucial fact is that admission to the American political community is and, under any imaginable circumstances, will remain a zero-sum game—a situation in which aliens must compete against one another for the very limited number of available admission slots—and it is not at all obvious that illegal aliens are the ones who should win it. The number of individuals who wish to come here vastly exceeds the number whom the society is prepared to admit. Refugee camps throughout the world are literally teeming with people for whom resettlement in the United States may be the only alternative to persecution or wretched, indefinite detention. State Department files are bursting with visa applications submitted years ago by people patiently waiting for their numbers to come up so that they can join family and friends or pursue a better life in the United States. Thousands of aliens from El Salvador, Haiti, and other nations, many of whom have risked their lives to reach our shores, are languishing in American jails awaiting asylum determinations or deportation.

All of these groups have moral and legal claims to admission and ultimately to political membership that are at least as compelling as those of most of the illegal aliens whose children are now guaranteed American citizenship by their birth here. Unless and until birthright citizenship for such children is explicitly embraced by Congress as a policy, then, this guaranteed membership will not only continue to offend the consensual principle upon which the legitimacy of American political identity must ultimately rest, but will also weaken other deeply felt moral commitments that must compete for realization by American society.

5 TOWARD A CONSENSUALIST LAW OF CITIZENSHIP: A PROPOSAL AND REPLY TO CRITICS

Three basic steps are required to achieve a law of citizenship at birth that is theoretically consistent, practical for addressing current policy problems, and consonant with the nation's fundamental claim that its government rests on the consent of the governed. The first step requires a reinterpretation of the Citizenship Clause of the Fourteenth Amendment. Its guarantee of citizenship to those born "subject to the jurisdiction" of the United States should be read to embody the public law's conception of consensual membership, and therefore to refer only to children of those legally admitted to permanent residence in the American community—that is, citizens and legal resident aliens.[1]

We have argued that this reinterpretation is legitimate in light of several factors: the theoretical ambivalence on the part of the Fourteenth Amendment's framers concerning the basis for citizenship; the inconsistencies that have always pervaded American citizenship law; the contemporary irrelevance of many of the reasons that led courts to perpetuate the medieval ascriptive principle in the past; and the existence of policy considerations today that increase the practical and theoretical attractiveness of the consensual principle. It is appropriate for the judiciary to adopt this reinterpretation because it is chiefly the judiciary that created the rival common-law understanding of political membership and defended it as authoritative, both before and after the adoption of the Citizenship Clause. Hence, a judicial reinterpretation is possible where, as here, its original reading of ambiguous language reflected policies and principles at variance with most contemporary views of American constitutional theory and with current national policy objectives.[2] This is especially true here, where no court has ever squarely decided the question of the status under the Citizenship Clause of the native-born children of illegal and nonimmigrant aliens.[3]

On our consensualist reading, those born "subject to the jurisdiction" of the United States would be citizens at birth provisionally, in the sense that they would have the opportunity upon attaining majority to renounce that citizenship if they so desired. At no time, however, would they be vulnerable to any denial of consent to their membership on the part of the state. Their parents would be understood to have obtained for the children, as a condition of the parents' own consent to citizenship, the guarantee that their children would enjoy all the rights of citizenship during their minority (with the usual age restrictions) and would possess an absolute right to assume full citizenship at their majority if they wished. While it is obviously a fiction to assign parents any conscious decision to insist on citizenship for their children as a condition of their own membership, it is much more improbable to suppose that parents would wish things to be otherwise should the choice be presented to them. And since children are as yet incapable of consent, reliance on the parent's preferences until a child reaches maturity is the only way that citizenship can plausibly be said to rest on actual personal volition.

Native-born children of legal resident aliens would also be provisional citizens at birth and during their minority and would enjoy the same right to expatriation. As we have seen, the public-law tradition was admittedly divided on whether resident aliens should be treated as having obtained a guarantee of citizenship for their children upon entry, or as having received merely the promise of their own resident alien status for them.[4] The abstract principle of consent alone, moreover, yields no obvious answer to this question. But in light of America's long-standing grant of citizenship to resident alien children, its historic tradition of openness, and the likelihood that the vast majority of such alien children could eventually acquire citizenship in other ways, we propose (following Burlamaqui but not Vattel) to treat the children of resident aliens equally with those of citizens in this regard.[5]

In this view, however, citizenship at birth would not be guaranteed to the native-born children of those persons— illegal aliens and "nonimmigrant" aliens—who have never received the nation's consent to their permanent residence within it. The nation cannot plausibly be said to have guaranteed to such persons citizenship for their children even tacitly, as a condition of the parents' entry into the polity. It either did not approve their entry at all (in the case of illegal aliens), or it did so on the understanding that they and their dependents would depart at some set time (in the case of nonimmigrants). In this connection, it is of some interest that even the citizenship law of the United Kingdom, from whose antecedents our common law of citizenship was originally derived, and which continues to adhere to the birthright citizenship principle, does not extend it to the native-born children of either illegal aliens or temporary resident aliens.[6] The same is true of other Western European countries.[7]

Since the proposed doctrine would require a reinterpretation of the Citizenship Clause, the change would be made prospectively, assuring citizenship to those born in the United States while the current understanding has been in effect. As we noted earlier, justice demands that the law honor the legitimate expectations raised by the existing reading of the clause, but that does not preclude a reinterpretation that would alter future expectations by aligning them with the meaning that the framers of the Clause would probably have intended had they anticipated the conditions that prevail today. Again, although we would not want this reinterpretation to make it easier for the United States to adopt harshly restrictive immigration policies, this deplorable result need not and should not follow.[8] If contemporary attitudes toward immigration are perhaps not as generous as they were in the early nineteenth century, neither are they as nativist or restrictive as they were even as recently as the 1950s.

In any event, Congress bears the ultimate responsibility for fashioning the structure of our immigration policy, and the role of birthright citizenship for the children of illegal and nonimmigrant aliens—the decision either to grant or withhold it—is obviously only a small piece of that structure. Congress must carefully weigh the moral claims of these children to membership relative to the claims of other groups, assessing the likely effects on illegal immigration of eliminating their present guarantee of citizenship, and considering how such a change should relate to the more comprehensive, systematic measures for reducing illegal immigration that we and others have proposed, including employer sanctions, enhanced border enforcement, and enlarged legal admissions quotas. Then, and only then, can Congress responsibly resolve the birthright citizenship question.

In the current state of knowledge, it is not at all obvious what the outcome of such a policy assessment would be. Employer sanctions and improved enforcement have been debated extensively during recent years; their advantages and disadvantages are by now reasonably well understood. Thus, for example, employer sanctions would weaken the magnet that attracts most undocumented workers here but would be difficult to enforce and could increase discrimination against Hispanic citizens and legal residents. Effective border enforcement might control the flow of illegal aliens near its source but probably could not be achieved at politically sustainable funding levels.

A policy of expanded legal admissions, however, has been less prominently discussed and deserves a few additional words. It is important to recall that, by historical standards, the number of new immigrants that even the more generous proposals for expanded admissions envision is quite small in proportion to the total population. (The effects of expanded admissions on the incentives for additional migration is a separate, more difficult question.) More than 14 percent of the United States population in 1910 was foreign-born compared to less than 5 percent in 1970. (Although these figures do not count illegal migrants, their inclusion would raise the total by only 1 or 2 percentage points.) In 1980, eight other industrialized countries had a higher percentage of foreign-born residents than the United States did.[9] Moreover, our population is aging rapidly, current fertility rates are quite low, and labor shortages loom. Legal immigrants unquestionably contribute a great deal to the American economy, culture, and society. In short, the prospect of even a million or more legal immigrants annually joining a nation of 236 million people should be cause for eager celebration, not for alarm. Even a return to the legal immigration total population ratio that prevailed during the 1920s, the decade in which the quota system was firmly established, would constitute a policy improvement.[10]

Our emphasis upon congressional power to define the contours of birthright citizenship is important. To insist on an automatic inclusiveness (in reality, *over*inclusiveness) by perpetuating the ascriptive principle in the Constitution, instead of by fully exposing immigration policies to public choice, is to betray a lack of confidence in the justice of consensual political self-definition that we believe is unwarranted today. It is doubtless true that if Americans gain full power to decide through normal democratic processes which aliens should be admitted to the national community, public debate over the issue will ventilate some of the mean-spirited nativistic sentiments that have always blighted American life.[11] But we believe that after the issues are fully explored, contemporary Americans will decide generously, and that those so admitted and naturalized will be treated as full and equal citizens.

On the other hand, maintaining the traditional interpretation of the clause will not eliminate such hostile attitudes; it will merely direct them toward different targets. If an increasing number of newcomers can, by means of illegal actions, claim political membership only because their parents have exploited an anachronistic understanding of the clause, then the society will be more likely to adopt harsh policies born of resentment and prejudice against such citizens, their noncitizen family members, and aliens in general. It would be wiser, we think, to confront hostility toward aliens initially over the questions of their admission and the status of their native-born children, rather than try to combat subsequent discriminatory impulses and measures partly fueled by the belief that many should not have been allowed to become citizens in the first place.

The second step necessary to realize a consistent, consensual law of citizenship at birth is to render the right of expatriation more meaningful. We propose that a formal procedure be established and publicized under which any citizen, at the age of majority, may expatriate himself. The right to do so already exists, of course, having been established by law in 1868. But despite recurring calls for legislation fully prescribing formal expatriation procedures, no regularly available domestic process has ever been established.[12] Currently, the attorney general is authorized to prescribe a means to renounce citizenship formally in time of war whenever he deems such renunciation not to be contrary to the interests of national defense. Moreover, a number of acts undertaken in foreign states—including naturalization, taking an oath of allegiance, or formally renouncing citizenship before a United States diplomatic or consular officer—are taken to constitute voluntary expatriation.[13] But, as noted above, there is no legislated procedure for expatriating oneself within the United States under more normal circumstances. As a result, few know that an expatriation right exists, and it is procedurally difficult to exercise. In that sense, citizenship is experienced more as ascribed than as consensual.

It should be eminently feasible to establish within some suitable governmental agency an inexpensive procedure for notifying all eligible persons at age eighteen that they may formally decline to accept the American citizenship that is their right.[14] Because no difficult factual or legal determinations would need to be made, administering the cases of those who did choose expatriation would be simple. The information should stress the implications of such a choice, and no affirmative action should be necessary in order for citizenship to vest. Failure to expatriate oneself formally and intentionally when provided the opportunity to do so should be taken as tacit consent to citizenship, just as it is today. That consent could be made all the more plausible by permitting those who did choose to renounce American citizenship to remain in the country as permanent resident aliens, with all the attendant rights and duties of that status, if they so desired. Hence, expatriation would not be forestalled by an inability to remove elsewhere.

This procedure may seem to invite expatriation, thereby raising the old fears concerning the effects of extensive self-expatriation on the stability of government. But it is extremely unlikely that many Americans would choose to expatriate themselves. Expatriation would sever the individual from important political privileges. If the person chose permanent resident status, as our proposal would permit, and

did not acquire a new nationality, he or she would be literally stateless.[15] Although the notorious vulnerability of
that condition would be reduced by the guarantee of permanent residence in the United States, expatriation would
remain, as it must and should be, an exceedingly difficult
choice.

It may appear, conversely, that our proposal would make
expatriation still too difficult, given that statelessness is such
an exceedingly undesirable condition. The procedure suggested here, however, would not only permit native-born
citizens to seek another nationality, but would also guarantee them permanent residence in the United States if they
wished it. The government could easily supply appropriate
travel documents indicating that the individual in question
is a permanent resident alien of the United States who cannot be denied readmission, thus mitigating most of the
worst consequences of statelessness.[16] While statelessness
would and should remain a problematic choice, we agree
with McDougal, Lasswell, and Chen that, in keeping with
"the overriding policy of honoring freedom of choice, there
would appear to be no reason why an individual should not
be allowed to render himself stateless, if the decision is freely
made, with full appreciation of the resultant consequences."[17]

Furthermore, under current American law, these permanent residents, if males, would still be obliged to perform
all the most burdensome duties of American citizens, including whatever military service might be required.[18] Hence,
the procedure would weaken the nation's military capabil-
ities only if large numbers chose not only to refuse American
citizenship but to relocate abroad, separating themselves
from their families and communities as well as from their

polity. The momentousness of such a course would undoubtedly discourage its pursuit. And if the expatriation
right appeared to be endangering the nation in a time of
war, the nation could insist, as it does at present, that the
right could not be exercised within the United States if it
were "contrary to the interests of national defense."[19] Such
limitations on expatriation, as well as military service requirements for permanent resident aliens, are disturbing,
however, for they imply that the nation does not believe
that a government that is genuinely "by the people" can
avoid perishing without imposing such nonconsensual and
illiberal restrictions.[20] They also render a choice to expatriate
oneself and to become a permanent resident alien largely
symbolic, since the most arduous burden of citizenship,
compulsory military service, remains. Nonetheless, for those
who wish to deny all claims of consent to full civic membership and to stress that their military service is indeed
essentially a product of coercion, the opportunity for even
this symbolic change in status may be of great significance.

Our proposal would also retain the previously noted
asymmetry, created by earlier Supreme Court rulings, between affirming the individual's right to self-expatriation,
while denying the nation's power to denationalize those who
are already members.[21] Although a thoroughgoing commitment to pure consensual membership might seem to
imply a national power to denationalize citizens at will, the
existence of such a power might threaten the vigorous exercise of basic constitutional freedoms, such as First Amendment political rights, or might create a condition of
involuntary statelessness and thus of acute human vulnerability. Our proposals, in contrast, are designed to leave

most individuals, including the native-born children of illegal aliens and those who voluntarily expatriate themselves,
with the nationality of their parents, while preserving the
possibility of relief and protection for those children whose
parents' nations refuse to recognize the children as their
citizens. Our proposals, therefore, could produce statelessness only for some individuals who knowingly chose that
status by voluntarily exercising their right of expatriation.

Our proposed constitutional interpretation, it should be
noted, leaves the status of naturalized citizens and so-called
statutory citizens, including children born abroad to at least
one American citizen, unaffected. Existing naturalization
law already expresses entirely consensualist premises; the
applicant gains naturalized citizenship by meeting the residency and other requirements set by the existing community, and by voluntarily avowing his or her own allegiance.[22]
As discussed above, moreover, the Citizenship Clause's ineradicably ascriptive element (qualified, as we have argued,
by a consensual one) requires that persons be born in the
United States to qualify for constitutional citizenship.[23] As
to all others, notably children born abroad to American
parents, the Constitution clearly leaves the question of citizenship—the scope of *jus sanguinus*—to Congress's discretion, a discretion that the Supreme Court has indicated is
quite broad.[24] We believe the requirement that in order to
be constitutionally mandated citizens, individuals must be
born within the geographic bounds of the United States,
cannot plausibly be discounted. Our interpretation, therefore, would leave the treatment of "statutory citizenship"
in American law intact.

We suggest, however, that Congress exercise its authority

over children born abroad to an American parent to take a
third step toward a more consensual law of citizenship. If
the Constitution permitted the public-law view to be followed completely, all children of American parents would
equally be guaranteed the option of choosing American citizenship if they so desired, regardless of their place of birth.
Congressional policy has in fact moved historically toward
this position, though this principle has never been entirely
fulfilled.[25] Currently, however, children born overseas automatically obtain statutory citizenship if they have at least
one American parent who has previously been resident in
the United States or its outlying possessions for a certain
period (which varies with the status of the spouse). Moreover, those children of American parents who are born overseas and do not obtain citizenship at birth have special
opportunities for subsequent naturalization.[26]

We do not insist that Congress must accord foreign-born
children of Americans identical rights to native-born children in all respects. Because the foreign-born are not similarly situated, some differences in treatment may be
appropriate even on consensualist premises. As argued earlier, no formal procedure for *electing* citizenship seems necessary for those who are born within the United States and
continue to reside here. By remaining in the United States
without choosing to expatriate themselves when given a
meaningful option to do so, they can plausibly be said to
have tacitly consented to membership. If a person born
overseas continues to reside there, however, such an inference of tacit consent is much less clearly warranted. Hence,
Congress might properly prescribe somewhat different conditions as necessary to support an inference of consent to

citizenship. Similarly, native-born Americans can expatriate themselves by undergoing naturalization or formally swearing allegiance to another country, while a person born overseas to American parents might never have occasion to do so, since he might be content with the foreign nationality ascribed to him by reason of his birth within that nation. Again, then, Congress might set different requirements for the acts that are deemed to constitute expatriation in the case of the foreign-born without violating an even-handed consensualism.

In general, however, we believe that the nation's policy should be to make citizenship an option guaranteed to all children of an American parent, whether born in or out of the United States. Admittedly, it may seem incongruous to guarantee citizenship to someone who lives his entire life outside the United States, while denying it to someone who resides for the same period of time within it, albeit illegally. That incongruity, however, is only apparent; the consent principle permits, even if it does not require, differential treatment of these two situations. Thus, a concern to implement the community's choice to exclude some groups is perfectly consistent with a consensual decision to accept the children of all existing members, whether or not those children subsequently decide to remain abroad. Under our proposal, moreover, any remaining incongruity would result only if the current American community chose it. Congress would have the power, if it wished, to require positive affirmations of membership on the part of those born to American parents residing overseas. Their continued citizenship would then be no more incongruous than allowing continued citizenship for native-born Americans who live abroad without renouncing their nationality. Finally, as we have emphasized, Congress would also have the right to admit all those living in the United States illegally or without citizenship to full political membership.[27] The relevant point, once again, is that the consensualist interpretation and policies that we propose would make the boundaries of the political community, for better or for worse, matters of self-conscious public choice.

Several plausible objections to our proposal for a more consensual citizenship law may be anticipated and deserve responses. Although there is something to be said for each of them, none seems decisive.

The first objection is textual in nature. It argues that the words of the Citizenship Clause of the Fourteenth Amendment literally preclude denying birthright citizenship to any individual who was "born in the United States" and is subject to its "jurisdiction." In this view, the clause's words are clear and comprehensive; they represent a deliberate constitutional decision to bestow citizenship on all who are native-born; they say nothing explicit about the parents' legal status or congressional consent, and they should not be interpreted as if they did.

This broad reading of the clause is not obviously incorrect or illegitimate; indeed, the Supreme Court seems to have endorsed this reading in its recent *Plyler* decision. Yet a number of considerations undermine this objection, and we think that they must be decisive in the end. First, it is simply wrong to assert that there has ever been a conscious deliberate decision, by the framers of the Fourteenth Amendment or its judicial interpreters, to accord birthright citizenship under the clause to children of illegal aliens. We saw in chapter 3 that the issue was not before the original framers of the Citizenship Clause; that the phrase "subject to the jurisdiction thereof," while ambiguous at best, suggests that they intended to grant the clause a scope narrower than universal citizenship for mere birth within the geographic United States; and that this phrase gave the clause a political and consensual meaning, not simply a legal and geographical one, that excluded several categories of individuals whom a purely geographic reading would have covered. Subsequently, as we saw in chapter 4, no Supreme Court decision—*Wong Kim Ark* and *Plyler* included—has ever faced the precise question posed by our proposal to limit birthright citizenship. Any claim that the nation has chosen to limit its consensual authority over political membership by constitutionally guaranteeing universal birthright citizenship must therefore proceed not from an appeal to the text, from explicit aims of the framers, or from authoritative judicial decisions, but rather from the hazier notion of "tacit consent."

This suggests a second line of criticism. It would accept the primacy of the consent principle in American political life but would argue that the long-standing acceptance of a broad birthright citizenship rule, coupled with the manifest ineffectiveness of current immigration enforcement efforts, should be understood as the political community's *tacit* consent to membership for the children born here of illegal alien parents.[28] That tacit consent, it might be argued, creates a moral obligation to continue a policy of universal birthright citizenship today.

We believe, however, that any argument from tacit consent should be viewed with skepticism,[29] and that this application of that argument is especially unconvincing. First, the inadequacy of immigration enforcement is not an unambiguous datum; it can only be properly evaluated in context. That context includes the inherent difficulty of the task (given the number of aliens who come and the ease of entering without detection) and the recent substantial increases in the INS's enforcement budget and in its apprehensions along the southern border.[30] *All* law enforcement is ineffective in that it is neither designed nor funded to bring each and every offender to justice. But that certainly does not mean—except in the most trivial sense—that society tacitly consents to those offenses that are not detected or prosecuted.

A second, more important defect in the argument from tacit consent is that it amounts to a reflexive acceptance and legitimation of the status quo. In contrast, this book is intended to reappraise the conventional understanding of birthright citizenship and to call into serious question its justification under contemporary conditions. Such scrutiny of established legal rules and institutions ought to be part of the democratic project. Instead of a consent defined by hypothesis and tautology, a democratic society should insist upon a consent exemplified by deliberate, self-conscious political choice. While we agree that the nation has certain obligations toward those who have been guided by the constitutional interpretations and public policies of the past, these should not preclude efforts to make the terms of national and individual consent as explicit as possible in the future. Our proposals are meant to accomplish this. In a polity in which actual consent is expressed symbolically only through periodic elections, these proposals can impart a new social meaning and integrity to the tacit consent that must suffice during the intervening periods.

A third objection might invoke the special character of constitutionally protected rights. It would insist that even if the nation, in adopting the Fourteenth Amendment, did not consciously or tacitly limit its future choices concerning citizenship, the definition of political membership remains so crucial to the nature of any polity that it should nevertheless be treated as an issue of constitutional dimension, one not subject to the whims and prejudices of transient majorities. Sustaining birthright citizenship for all native-born as a constitutional guarantee might be seen as a way to safeguard basic national values against temporary aberrations, as is done for free speech and other basic rights.

The weakness in this argument is that it ignores the basic difference between a right that a community decides to safeguard for members and nonmembers against popular majorities, and a claimed right to *become* a member. The latter claim, if recognized, would limit a nation's very power to determine what it will be—and also to determine who will decide that question—in the future. The current dilemma created by the influx of illegal aliens suggests that if these choices cannot be made on a flexible, ongoing basis, they cannot be made at all.

Furthermore, insofar as the Constitution does explicitly indicate how questions of membership are to be decided, it does so by granting Congress power over immigration, naturalization, and expatriation. These powers establishing congressional authority over which individuals may enter the United States can best be understood as expressing the framers' concern to ensure that all individuals "born in the United States" will be born to parents who are present with the consent of the nation. These powers therefore imply an open-ended, consensual process permitting the redefinition of the nation's membership. Because our constitutional system thus generally remits questions of admission to membership to majoritarian processes, and because this course is most consistent with the nation's fundamental commitment to consent, we believe that the Citizenship Clause should be read in that spirit.

Fourth, it may be argued that our interpretation of the jurisdiction requirement loses the administrative clarity and simplicity of the current birthright citizenship rule. Clarity and simplicity are unquestionably important virtues in a citizenship test. America's experiences under the Alien and Sedition Act and with loyalty investigations during the McCarthy era are grim reminders, if any were needed, that individualized inquiries into the delicate, often ineffable questions of loyalty and political allegiance can be oppressive and dangerous. Our proposal, however, would avoid such intrusion through the presumption, conclusive against the government, that all native-born individuals whose parents were citizens or legal permanent residents at the time of birth would automatically acquire citizenship unless they formally renounced it upon reaching majority. The simplicity of the current rule, we maintain, is the simplicity of over-breadth; it confers irrevocable citizenship upon many individuals from whom, according to consensualist principles, it could be withheld. In doing so, it also engenders complex problems of dual citizenship that belie its claims

to simplicity.[31] Our proposal would continue the current
rule's administrative workability while avoiding the dual
citizenship morass for those born here of alien parents.

Fifth, it may be argued that the proposal is not as inclusive
as the current rule, and that inclusiveness, like administrative simplicity, is a great advantage in a citizenship test.
There can be no doubt that inclusiveness is especially important for a society that prides itself on its openness to
immigrants and its liberality of spirit toward all those in
need. We share that pride and are strongly committed to a
genuinely inclusive political community. Again, we recognize that, over and above the formalities of consent, those
who have been born and grown up within the United States
often become in fact part of the actual, organic community
that is produced by shared experiences, so that refusing
them membership in the only community they really know
may seem objectionable on grounds of liberal humanitarianism or territoriality. That is why we have proposed admission for all those who have been born in the United
States under the current interpretation of the Citizenship
Clause, and why we call for Congress to assess the value of
such a change to an effective immigration policy.

We are convinced, however, that not even the most ardent
advocates of a liberal immigration policy favor *universal*
inclusiveness; few would dispute that the citizens of a nation
have some right to shape their collective futures by con-
trolling admissions. The real question, therefore, is what
the appropriate principle of inclusion (or exclusion) ought
to be, recognizing that a less-than-universal principle of
inclusion must inevitably also exclude, and that exclusion
must inevitably nullify some individuals' choices for mem-

bership. By confining citizenship at birth to children of citizens or legal permanent residents, levels of illegal immigration might be reduced, thereby lessening the problem of what to do about those who have long been in the midst of the community, albeit illegally. This reduction in illegal migration seems particularly likely if our birthright citizenship proposal were part of a broader program to discourage illegal immigration. If the nation adopted these measures but found that they did not diminish the number of children born of illegal alien parents who had spent most of their lives here and had acquired humanitarian claims to membership, Congress would retain the power to extend a generous amnesty or naturalization policy toward them.

That residual power, of course, would not guarantee as inclusive a policy as the existing birthright citizenship rule does. But the current rule achieves an inclusiveness that is both spurious and uncontrolled. It is spurious because it is based upon a purely geographical concidence—literally an accident of birth—rather than upon a principle, such as consent, that can legitimate citizenship by making it conform to the moral and political presuppositions of the national community. Birthright citizenship's inclusiveness of membership is also uncontrolled because it abdicates what is perhaps the most fundamental question of our political life—who shall constitute "we the people"? Rather than squarely addressing that question as one that should be decided deliberately on moral and policy grounds by the national community, it leaves it to the self-interested decisions of those over whom we have no effective control.

Our proposal, in contrast, promises a more genuine inclusiveness. Being grounded in actual, explicit consent, the

inclusiveness would be more legitimate, more truly reflec-
tive of national sentiment, than the current rule. It would
be as generous (or as niggardly) as Americans self-consciously decided to make it. As suggested earlier, an immigration and citizenship policy that is widely perceived
as being under the nation's direction and rooted in its consent seems far more likely to be generously inclusive than
a policy, like the present one, that is viewed as abdicating
control and violating national will. Although we do not
contend that the proposal could achieve that result itself,
it would almost certainly contribute to its eventual
realization.

Sixth, it may be argued, in a somewhat similar vein, that
the proposal does little to address the problem of the influx
and status of illegal aliens. Indeed, by eliminating birthright
citizenship for their native-born children, the proposal could
(depending upon the magnitude of its countervailing dis-
incentives to illegal migration) actually increase the number
of individuals in illegal status. In this view, the current
birthright citizenship rule has at least one virtue that our
proposal lacks. It recognizes that in fact (due largely to
ineffective immigration enforcement) many native-born
children of illegal aliens, along with their parents, will successfully elude detection or avoid deportation and remain
here indefinitely. Denying birthright citizenship to those
children would add one more obstacle and disadvantage,
one more source of stigma and discrimination, to those they
must endure as they continue living in American society, as
many will be able to do. This dilemma is compounded by
the fact that these children's life prospects would be clouded
by the action of others over whom they have no control—

in this case, the illegal entry of their parents.[32] Better (so defenders of the current rule might argue) to eliminate their cruel disability at the moment of birth than to maintain it thereafter.[33]

Although superficially appealing, this argument from life prospects is ultimately unpersuasive. Our proposal to make one's national status turn, at least provisionally, on the national status of one's parents seems more morally acceptable and less determinative of one's life prospects than many other contingent factors—such as inherited wealth, upbringing, or genetic endowment—that are far more likely to shape those prospects in fundamental ways. Indeed, our proposal seems less arbitrary in terms of life prospects than the fundamental concept of birthright citizenship itself, which bases national status wholly upon the accident of geographical location at birth. And even if the innocence of the child and allied concern for his life prospects are accepted as morally or legally relevant, it does not follow that *citizenship*, as distinguished from mere nondiscrimination, should be the prize for that innocence. Nondiscrimination does not necessarily imply the same rights and benefits that citizenship or legal residence status confers.[34] These children and their parents, by being denied birthright citizenship, would not be treated as the *Dred Scott* decision treated blacks; they would not be denied the law's protection. They would merely be required to choose among continuing to live in illegal status, with more limited equal protection and due process rights; seeking to obtain legal status; or returning to their home countries.

A seventh objection, aimed at our expatriation proposal, is suggested in an essay by Michael Walzer, in which he considers an option much like the one proposed here. Walzer considers permitting persons at majority explicitly to choose to become, in Walzer's phrase, "resident aliens at home,"[35] only to reject that option on the ground that it compels "very young men" to make a "very difficult" and, he assumes, permanent choice. He argues instead that "alienated residents" should retain citizenship while being treated like conscientious objectors in regard to the greatest demand of citizenship, compulsory military service, and he opposes conscription entirely except under threat of national "devastation."[36]

Those suggestions, however, appear much more objectionable than the present proposal, for they would require some procedure by which young men (at least) could identify themselves as "alienated" but still citizens, thus winning a virtually costless exemption from civic obligations sustained by others. And Walzer's initial concerns appear misplaced: young persons already have the option of expatriation, and our proposal would only make that choice better informed and more concrete, though certainly not costless. Nor would it inevitably involve a permanent loss of all opportunity for citizenship. The choice of criteria for admission of such expatriate resident aliens, as with all aliens, would remain with Congress and hence be subject to popular control. It is true that the nation might well be reluctant to readmit to citizenship those who have expatriated themselves to avoid certain types of military service. But the nation has often been lenient toward such persons, as in the amnesty eventually granted to many Vietnam-era draft evaders,[37] and it is likely to be so in the aftermath of any unpopular military venture. It remains true that such le-

niency would not be guaranteed, so that the choice to expatriate oneself would be very difficult. But that difficulty
inheres, as it should, in making citizenship genuinely and
mutually consensual. Indeed, the difficulty exists quite as
fully at present, obscured only by the fact that American
law now makes the choice of expatriation procedurally and
substantively demanding.

Finally, it might be argued that our proposals would have
little practical effect. The current system, by combining
birthright citizenship with a very broad right of expatriation, might seem to be tantamount to a citizenship based
upon consent because any individual can withdraw consent
at any time simply by expatriating himself. Since we have
already considered this argument, it need not long detain
us. As we explained, birthright citizenship-cum-expatria-
tion is not a proxy for mutual consent; thus, it fundamentally differs from our program in principle.[38] In practice, of
course, our proposals would have important effects. They
would eliminate constitutionally guaranteed birthright citizenship prospectively for the native-born children of illegal
and nonimmigrant aliens; create a usable, formal expatriation procedure; expand statutory citizenship; increase the
number of aliens admitted under legal quotas; and enhance
the effectiveness of immigration enforcement.

If these proposals accomplished nothing else, moreover,
they would at least demonstrate that the nation takes seriously its long-professed commitment to resting political
membership upon genuine, mutual consent. In a more consensualist system like the one we propose, the idea of tacit
consent, although always problematic, could be taken as a
relatively plausible, realistic account of the individual's cur-

rent disposition toward the polity. That crucially important idea could not as readily serve, as it does today under the ascriptive conception of birthright citizenship, as an ideological fig leaf that conceals the nakedness of the polity's presumptions of active consent and legitimacy. The government of a more truly consensual polity could more truthfully proclaim to citizens, resident aliens, and illegal aliens alike that American citizenship stands on a firm foundation of freely willed membership. It could more credibly claim the contemporaneous allegiance and, if necessary, the personal sacrifice of its citizens than it was able to do during the Vietnam War and other corrosive national conflicts. It could more persuasively invoke what it now can only baldly assert—a legitimacy grounded in a fresh, vital, and always revocable consent.

NOTES

Introduction

1. Art. I, Sec. 8 did authorize Congress to "establish a uniform Rule of Naturalization." That citizenship was regarded by the Founders as a significant legal and political status is suggested by the fact that citizenship is mentioned, as Justice Rehnquist has observed, "in no less than 11 instances in a political document noted for its brevity." *Sugarman v. Dougall*, 413 U.S. 634, 651–52 (1973) (dissenting opinion). United States citizenship is mentioned three times in the original Constitution. See Art. I, Sec. 2; Art. 2, Sec. 3; Art. II, Sec. 1.

2. See *infra* chap. 2 at notes 60–78 and accompanying text.

3. Amend. XIV, Sec. 1.

4. For a discussion of contrasting views on this question, see V. Briggs, Jr., *Immigration Policy and the American Labor Force* (1984).

5. For example, A. Leibowitz, "The Acquisition of Citizenship: Jus soli v. Jus Sanguinis," 3 *Federal Immigration Law Reporter* 10–13 (April 15, 1985), appears to assume that the birthright citizenship guarantee extends to children of illegal aliens but does not explicitly address the issue. See also our discussion of *Plyler v. Doe* on this point, *infra* at chap. 4, notes 37–42 and accompanying text.

Chapter 1

1. As will be evident in the discussion *infra*, the principles of political membership by ascription and membership by consent can each be viewed (under certain assumptions, and with varying plau-

sibility) as consistent with laws deriving citizenship from place of birth and from descent. Nevertheless, citizenship by ascription accords most naturally with citizenship by birthplace, while line of descent is more useful as an element of a practical law of consensual membership.

2. M. Walzer *The Revolution of the Saints*, 148–71 (1965).

3. Sir A. Cockburn, *Nationality: or the Law relating to Subjects and Aliens considered with a View to Future Legislation*, 7 (1869).

4. *Id.* at 7–8; J. Kettner, *The Development of American Citizenship 1608–1870*, 13–15 (1978).

5. *Id.* at 7, 15–17; *Calvin's Case*, 7 Co. Rep. la (1608).

6. Coke remained concerned to preserve the authority of courts and parliaments against royal absolutism. See, e.g., Black, "The Constitution of Empire: The Case for the Colonists," 124 *U. of Pa. L. Rev.* 1179–1211 (1976).

7. Kettner, *id.* at 17.

8. *Id.* at 45.

9. *Calvin's Case*, 7 Co. Rep. 15b (1608).

10. "Ligeance and obedience is an incident inseparable to every subject, for as soon as he is born he oweth birthright ligeance and obedience to his sovereign." *Id.* at 4b.

11. In regard to any particular sovereign, Coke wrote, each man "was either Alienigena, an Alien born, or Subditus, a Subject born." *Id.* at 17a.

12. Coke stated that it was "neither the climate nor the soil, but ligeantia and obedietia that make the Subject born"; there was thus no allegiance owed to "England it self, taking it for the Continent thereof." *Id.* at 6a, 11b–12a.

13. *Id.* at 18a.

14. Kettner, *supra* note 4, at 23.

15. While Coke wrote that those born "under the obedience, power, faith, ligealty, or ligeance of the King, are natural Subjects," he subsequently specified that "power and protection draweth ligeance." *Id.* at 5b, 9b.

16. *Id.* at 18a–18b.

17. *Id.* at 14b, 16b.

18. *Id.* at 6a.

19. *Id.* at 5b, 8a, 13a–13b.

20. *Id.* at 4a.

21. Walzer *supra* note 2 at 153, 156; Kettner, *supra* note 4 at 19.

22. Coke expressed these assumptions when he argued that it is according to "the law of God and Nature" that the "ligeance and obedience of the subject" is "due to his sovereign or superior" *Calvin's Case*, 7 Co. Rep. 13a (1608). In the same vein, Filmer argued that "civil power" existed "by divine institution," so that even when kings appeared to have been selected by the lords or the people, "he that is so elected claims not his power as a donative from the people, but as being substituted properly by God, from whom he receives his royal charter of an universal father, though testified by the ministry of the heads of the people." See R. Filmer, *Patriarcha*, in T. I. Cook, ed., *Two Treatises of Government*, 255, 259 (1956)

23. Michael Walzer indicates that, in addition to appealing to the hierarchical chain of being and to the ordering of the family, there was a third way in which medieval thought identified political life with the natural world: by viewing the body politic as a living organism. Somewhat surprisingly, perhaps, this line of argument does not appear to have been used extensively in analyzing the nature of political membership. Walzer, *supra* note 2 at 149, 171, 183.

24. Filmer, *id.* at 255, 258–60. This contention further requires that the father be viewed as having unlimited natural dominion over his children. As discussed *infra*, Filmer and other defenders of monarchical absolutism in England and abroad also made this claim. *Id.* at 265; Walzer, *id.* at 183, 185.

25. James Kettner notes, for example, that Coke's insistence on the irrevocable, natural status of one's allegiance to the sovereign of one's birthplace is understandable if we observe that while one can acquire an adoptive father or stepfather, nothing can alter the identity of one's natural father. Kettner, *id.* at 8, 18–19, 23, 41–43.

26. See *infra* notes 39–45 and accompanying text; J. Fliegelman, *Prodigals and Pilgrims*, 4, 12–15 (1982); N. Tarcov, *Locke's Education for Liberty* (1984), 4–5, 57–76.

27. *Calvin's Case*, 7 Co. Rep. 3b–5b, 8a, 13b, 25a (1608).

28. Even traitors and outlaws were entitled to royal protection from private vengeance prior to their legal punishment. *Id.* at 13b–14b.

29. *Id.* at 13b, 25a.

30. Patriarchs could choose "to remit some part of their fatherly authority." Filmer, *supra* note 22, at 255, 260, 265, 279, 281–82, 289–90.

31. Walzer *supra* note 2 at 189.

32. Filmer, *id.* at 255, 259–60, 265, 281–83.

33. Coke said that while a man who exercised wardship over a child through "seignory" was required to forfeit that wardship to the king from whom he received it should he be exiled, a father was entitled to retain his natural wardship over his child in such circumstances. *Calvin's Case*, 7 Co. Rep. 136 (1608). Whether the king could override the father's natural authority in the name of his own sovereignty over a child that was a natural-born subject, Coke did not consider in *Calvin's Case*. His defense of natural sovereignty, however, almost certainly implies the existence of that power.

34. See *infra* Chap. 4 notes 14–15; chap. 5, notes 5–7, 31–32 and accompanying text.

35. See *supra* notes 17–19, 30–33 and accompanying text.

36. J. Locke, *Two Treatises of Government*, 389 (rev. ed., 1965).

37. For doubts about the influence of Locke's *Second Treatise*, see J. Dunn, "The Politics of Locke in England and America," *in* J. W. Yolton, ed., *John Locke: Problems and Perspectives*, 78 (1969); Pocock, *infra* note 38, at 423–24; G. Wills, *Inventing America*, 169–75 (1978). For a reaffirmation of Locke's significance, see J. P. Diggins, *The Lost Soul of American Politics* (1984). Even if correct, however, the doubts do not undermine the significance of Locke's political and moral ideas for early American thought, because those ideas are also contained in others of Locke's works, notably his *Essay concerning the Human Understanding*, *Letter concerning Toleration*, and *Thoughts concerning Education*. No one disputes that these works were very widely read and influential in America. See, e.g., B. Bailyn, *The Ideological Origins of the American Revolution*, 27–30 (1967); H. May, *The Enlightenment in America*, 7–10, 38 (1976); Wills, *id.* at 170–71, 181–82; M. White, *The Philosophy of the American Revolution*, 64–65 (1978); Kettner, *supra* note 4 at 44–61; N. Wood, *The Politics of Locke's Philosophy*, 1–7 (1983); Fliegelman, *supra* note 26 at 12–15. Fliegelman notes that Locke's *Education* was the most widely read of all Locke's works and played a leading role in reshaping eighteenth-century America's conceptions of partriarchal power, both directly and through popular novels that took the reordering of familial relations as their theme. Fliegelman observes that this, in turn, had significant political impact in America: "Whig rhetoric and ideology in the decade between 1765 and 1775 drew extensively on the language and arguments of the familial contractualism that Locke had popularized." *Id.* at 98.

38. J. G. A. Pocock, *The Machiavellian Moment* (1975).

39. Locke held, however, that wives ordinarily were and should be subordinate to their husbands. Locke, *Two Treatises*, 209–10, 364.

40. *Id*. at 314, 345–61.

41. *Id*. at 352–53.

42. *Id*. at 312–14.

43. E.g., *id*. at 441.

44. *Id*. at 391–92. Professor Amar points out that this view of the inability of the child meaningfully to affirm his or her consent found parallels in the spiritual realm in the Anabaptist movement's opposition to infant baptism and in the insistence by other religions upon ritual affirmations or confirmations at more mature ages.

45. *Id*. at 358–61, 391–92.

46. *Id*. at 280–81, 380–88; M. Seliger, "Locke, Liberalism, and Nationalism," in J. W. Yolton, ed., *Locke: Problems and Perspectives*, 20–23 (1969).

47. Pocock, *supra* note 38.

48. For a recent critique of Pocock's stronger claims and a reassertion of the significance of Locke as well as Calvinism, see Diggins, *supra* note 37.

49. See J. J. Rousseau, *The Social Contract* (1968).

50. Montesquieu, *The Spirit of the Laws*, 37 (1949).

51. See *id*. at 69–70; Rousseau, *id*. at 69–70, 96, 186–87; J. J. Rousseau, *The Government of Poland*, 4, 8, 11, 13–14 (1972); *Politics and the Arts*, 123–37 (1960).

52. Aristotle, *Politics* 109 (1968).

53. Rousseau, *Government of Poland*, 20.

54. Rousseau, *id*. at 80–81; Montesquieu, *id*. at 138–39, 247.

55. Machiavelli, *Discourses*, 129–30 (1950).

56. Pocock, *supra* note 38 at 491, 492.

57. Aristotle, *supra* note 52 at 93, 198; Edmund S. Morgan, *American Slavery, American Freedom*, 380–87 (1975).

58. For discussion of various sorts of claims that territorial presence does create a right to membership, see *infra* chap. 1 at notes 76–77; chap. 4, notes 25–26; chap. 5, notes 28–32 and accompanying text.

59. For an analysis of this tension in early liberal thought, see R. M. Smith, *Liberalism and American Constitutional Law*, 36–38, 42–45 (1985).

60. *Id*. at 27–31, 37, 93.

61. Locke, *Two Treatises*, 454–77, esp. 462–64.

62. For a discussion of the meaning and contemporary significance of the distinction between expatriation and denationalization, see Comment, "Dual Nationality and the Problem of Expatriation," 16 *U.S.F.L. Rev.* 291, 292, n. 9 (1982).

63. Locke did at one point contemplate the possibility that a subject might be cut off from membership by "some public Act," but whether he was referring to a broad government power to denationalize members at will, a form of punishment, or an improper sovereign abrogation of the social contract is ambiguous. *Id.* at 394.

64. To Locke, even express allegiance could, however, be abrogated by the dissolution of the government or the unspecified "public Acts" that apparently could produce denationalization. *Id.* at 393-94.

65. *Id.* at 389-90.

66. *Id.* at 390-91, 393-94.

67. J. Locke, *An Essay concerning the Human Understanding*, 70-71, 349, 353-57 (Clarendon ed., 1975).

68. Godwin attacked the belief that because "men derived their existence from an infinite creator at first, so are they still subject to his providential care, and of consequence owe allegiance to their civil governors, as to a power which he has thought fit to set over them." He did so on the Lockean ground that the "criterion of patriarchal descent will be of no avail till the true claimant and rightful heir can be discovered."
W. Godwin, *An Enquiry concerning Political Justice*, 211 (1976).

69. *Id.* at 213. Godwin's dismissal of obligations stemming from the father's participation in the social contract was a rejection of the efforts by public-law theorists to make consensual membership more practical, as discussed *infra* chap. 2, notes 7-9, 11-14 and accompanying text.

71. *Id.* at 229-30, 234.

72. If it appeared, for example, that the child would "live with greater benefit under the superintendence of a stranger," the fact that someone else was his natural father was, to Godwin, "of no consequence." And while some deference of a child to his elders might be due because of their capacity to benefit him, that deference became "vicious" if there was reason to think that the parent had no "essential information" to impart to his offspring. *Id.* at 233-34, 246.

73. See, e.g., M. Walzer, *Obligations* (1970); M. McDougal, H. D. Lasswell, and L. Chen, *Human Rights and World Public Order*, 863-865 (1980).

74. M. Walzer, *Spheres of Justice* (1983), 32, 39, 61–62; McDougal, *id.* at 864.

75. See, e.g., McDougal, Lasswell, Chen, *id.* at 451.

76. *Id.* at 864.

77. For such communitarian perspectives in moral philosophy, see e.g., Walzer *supra* note 74 at xiv, 31–63; M. Sandel, "The Procedural Republic and the Unencumbered Self," 12 *Political Theory* 90–95 (1984). For a discussion of the increasing integration of that perspective into American public and private law, see Schuck, "The Transformation of Immigration law," 84 *Col. L. Rev.* 1, 34–90 (1984).

Chapter 2

1. Sir W. Blackstone, *Commentaries on the Laws of England* (facsimile of 1st ed., 1979).

2. H. Grotius, *De Jure Belli ac Pacis Libri Tres*, 1st ed. (1625).

3. S. Puffendorf, *De Jure naturae et gentium*, 1st ed. (1672).

4. J. J. Burlamaqui, *The Principles of Natural and Politic Law*, 4th ed. (1792).

5. E. de Vattel, *The Law of Nations; or, Principles of the Law of Nature: Applied to the Conduct and Affairs of Nations and Sovereigns* (1787).

6. Blackstone, *id.* at 357.

7. Kettner, *supra* chap. 1, note 4 at 54–55.

8. Burlamaqui argued specifically that: "the first founder of a state, and all those who afterwards became members thereof, are supposed to have stipulated, that their children and descendants should, at their coming into the world, have the right of enjoying those advantages which are common to all the members of the state, provided nevertheless that these descendants, when they attain to the use of reason are on their part willing to submit to the government, and to acknowledge the authority of the sovereign." Burlamaqui assumed that the political membership of the wife would always be identical to that of her husband, her "domestic governor," although he conceded that the laws of particular governments might differ on this point. Burlamaqui, *id* at 213–14.

9. Burlamaqui argued that if "the children of members of the state, upon attaining to the years of discretion, are willing to live in the place of their parentage, or in their native country, they are by

this very act supposed to submit themselves" to the appropriate sovereign. Burlamaqui's contrast of "place of parentage" and "native country" suggests that he believed that the "place of parentage" should and would extend the opportunity for membership to the children of resident aliens. *Id*. at 214.

10. *Id*. at 267–68.

11. Vattel, *supra* note 5 at 166, 168. Unlike Locke and Burlamaqui, Vattel argued that a child's political identity provisionally follows that of the father, not both parents. He did so because while he continued to accept considerable natural authority of the male over his wife and children, he no longer assumed that the wife automatically acquired the political identity of her husband at marriage. Vattel agreed, however, that these were matters that positive law could legitimately order differently. Vattel, *id*. at 167–68, 274–75; cf. Locke, *Two Treaties*, *supra* chap. 1, note 36 at 209–10, 352–53, 364.

12. Vattel, *id*. at 166–67.

13. *Id*.

14. *Id*. at 170.

15. *Id*. at 170–73.

16. In fact, the distinction between exile and banishment was that banishment alone imposed a "mark of infamy." *Id*. at 174–76.

17. Vattel, *id*. at 176.

18. *Id*. at 176–77; see also 263, 265, 278–79, 284, 285. At 265, Vattel suggests that, like Locke, he hopes the tension between consensual authority and human rights can generally be resolved in practice by a people's willingness to use its consensual powers to promote those rights. He states: "It is the same with respect to all rights; the proprietor may freely use them, and he does no injury to any person by making use of them; but if he would be free from all guilt and keep his conscience pure, he will never make any other use of them, but such as is most comfortable to his duty."

19. *Id*. at 95; Burlamaqui, *supra* note 4, at 103.

20. Vattel, *id*. at 168, 172.

21. While favoring a temperate patriotism, Washington and other revolutionary statesmen stressed that the true aspiration of Americans should not be to perfect their republic alone but to realize the "great republic of humanity at large." Fliegelman, *supra* chap. 1, note 26, at 227–30.

22. See *supra* Introduction, note 1 and accompanying text. The framers' only extended discussion of issues that involved citizenship

concerned the naturalization power and the periods of residency that should be required before naturalized citizens were eligible for federal office. M. Farrand, *Records of the U.S. Federal Convention of 1787*, 2:216, 235–39; Kettner, *supra* chap. 1, note 4, at 224, 226.

23. U.S. Constitution, Article II, Sec. I, cl. 4.

24. *Id.*; Kettner, *id.* at 231.

25. A. Hamilton, J. Madison, J. Jay, *The Federalist Papers*, 152 (1961).

26. M. D. Petersen, ed., *The Portable Thomas Jefferson*, 125 (1975).

27. F. G. Franklin, *The Legislative History of Naturalization in the United States*, 38, 52 (1906).

28. Kettner, *id.* at 173–85.

29. *Id.* at 189–209.

30. *Id.* at 184–87, 204–08.

31. As late as 1813, for example, Chief Justice Theophilus Parsons held in Massachusetts that during the Revolution the states had succeeded to the king's sovereignty after he had effectively abdicated by violating the social contract. But Parsons insisted that citizens of the new states, like subjects at common law, owed allegiance perpetually, unless the government consented to a change of nationality. *Ainslie v. Martin*, 9 Mass. 456–61 (1813); Kettner, *id.* at 191–92, 202–07.

32. See, e.g., J. Roche, "The Expatriation Cases," in P. Kirkland, ed., *The Supreme Court Review* 328 (1964); *Lynch v. Clarke*, 1 Sandford 583, 659 (N.Y. 1844).

33. Kettner, *id.* at 248–49, 267–68; Roche, *id.* at 329.

34. See, e.g., *Fish v. Stoughton*, 2 Johns. Cas. 407, 408 (N.Y. 1801); *Ainslie v. Martin*, 9 Mass. 454 (1813); *Coxe v. Gulick*, 5 Halstead 328, 331 (N.J. 1829); *Lynch v. Clarke*, 1 Sandford 583, 673 (N.Y. 1844).

35. Kettner, *id.* at 269–70; I. Tsiang, *The Question of Expatriation in America Prior to 1907*, 45–61 (1942).

36. Kettner, *id.* 15 267–75; Blackstone, *supra* note 1, at 357.

37. *Talbot v. Jansen*, 3 Dallas 133, 140–41, 150, 162 (1795).

38. *Id.* at 153, 162–63, 169.

39. Kettner, *id.* at 272.

40. For state cases, see, e.g., *Murray v. M'Carty*, 2 Munford 393 (Virginia, 1811) at 396–97; *Alsberry v. Hawkins*, 9 Dana 177 (Kentucky, 1839) at 178; but cf. *Kilham v. Ward*, 2 Mass. 236 (1806) at 237–38; *Ainslie v. Martin*, 9 Mass. 454 (1813) at 458–60. For federal cases, see, e.g., *M'Ilvaine v. Coxe's Lessee*, 4 Cranch 209 (1808) at 213; *Dawson's Lessee v. Godfrey*, 4 Cranch 321 (1808) at 323; *Inglis v. Sailor's Snug Harbor*, 3 Pet. 99 (1830); *Shanks v. DuPont* 3 Pet. 242

(1830). For overviews, see Tsiang, *supra* note 35, at 28–37, 41–43, 61–70; Kettner, *id.* at 267–84.

41. Tsiang, *id.* at 47, 60–61; Kettner, *id.* at 269–71.

42. 3 Pet. 99 (1830).

43. *Id.* at 173.

44. *Id.* at 159; *Shanks* v. *DuPont*, 3 Pet. 242, 245–46 (1830). This view of the interstitial role of natural law was widely held in the antebellum judiciary. See R. Cover, *Justice Accused: Antislavery and the Judicial Process* (1975).

45. 1 Sandford 583, 663 (N.Y. 1844).

46. *Id.* at 587–88.

47. *Id.* at 594–95.

48. *Id.* at 596.

49. *Id.* at 598. Kent's comment appears in *Commentaries on American Law* 2:33, 1st ed. (1827). See also 37, 42, where Kent essentially upholds the common-law view of expatriation.

50. *Id.* at 599.

51. *Id.*

52. *Id.* at 611–13.

53. *Id.* at 640–46, 652, 654–55.

54. *Id.* at 655–56, 664.

55. *Id.* at 658.

56. *Id.* at 657–73.

57. *Id.* at 673–74.

58. Tsiang, *supra* note 35 at 113.

59. Roche, *supra* note 32 at 335–36; R. Gray, "Expatriation—A Concept in Need of Clarification," 8 *U. C. Davis L. Rev.* 377–78, 388 (1975).

60. The Court also had to explain why women should be considered citizens but nonetheless should be denied political equality. It met this problem with the doctrine of "separate but equal" domestic and public spheres for the sexes. See, e.g., *Bradwell* v. *State*, 16 Wall. 130 (1872); *Minor* v. *Happersett*, 21 Wall. 162 (1875); and A. Sachs and J. H. Wilson, *Sexism and the Law*, 81–112 (1978).

61. Kettner, *supra* chap. 1, note 4 at 292–93, 297, 300.

62. *Id.* at 288–300.

63. 20 Johns. Repts. 693, 703 (N.Y. 1823).

64. *Id.* at 711–12.

65. *The Cherokee Nation* v. *State of Georgia*, 5 Peters 1, 17 (1831).

66. *Worcester* v. *Georgia*, 6 Peters 515, 552, 561 (1832).

67. Kettner, *id*. at 299–300.

68. *Id*. at 301, 311.

69. *Annals of Congress*, 16th Cong., 2d sess., 1820–21, at 599. While Hemphill's position was unassailable from a purely ascriptive perspective, he in fact rejected the "feudal" understanding of birthright citizenship as "slavish," and instead interpreted citizenship as "in the nature of a compact, expressly or tacitly made" (*Id*). It is likely, therefore, that he thought of the guarantee of birthright citizenship in Vattel's terms—as a right promised to parents on behalf of their children when they contracted to become members of a state.

70. *Id*. at 86–87 (Sen. John Holmes), 94 (Sen. H. Gray Otis), 546 (Cong. Philip Barbour), 585 (Cong. William Archer).

71. *Id*. at 555, 557 (Smyth), 615 (McLane).

72. *Id*. at 1129, 1134.

73. *Id*. at 86–87, 585, 615

74. Kettner, *id*. at 315–17.

75. *Id*. at 317–20.

76. *Amy (a woman of colour) v. Smith*, 1 Little 326 (1822).

77. *Id*. at 332.

78. *Id*. at 333.

79. Tsiang, *supra* note 35, at 86–88.

80. See *infra* chap. 3, notes 4–7, 12–25 and accompanying text.

Chapter 3

1. *Dred Scott v. Sanford*, 60 U.S. 393 (1857).

2. *Id*.

3. *Id*. at 407.

4. See, e.g., *id*. at 572–88 (Curtis, J. dissenting).

5. A. Cockburn, *supra* chap. 1, note 3 at 194.

6. Chapter 31, 14 Stat. 27 (April 9, 1866).

7. *Id*., Section 1.

8. Reprinted at *Cong. Globe*, 39th Cong., 1st sess., 1857–60 (1866) (hereafter *Globe*).

9. Art. I, Sec. 8.

10. E.g., *Globe* at 475, 497–98 (January 29, 1866) (remarks of Senator Peter Van Winkle); 499–500 (January 30, 1866) (remarks of Senator Edgar Cowan); 523-24 (January 31, 1866) (remarks of Senator Garrett Davis).

11. See, e.g., colloquy between Senators James Doolittle, William Fessenden, and Jacob Howard, at *Globe* at 2896–97 (May 30, 1866).

12. *Globe* at 474 (January 29, 1866).

13. *Globe* at 498 (January 30, 1866).

14. Text accompanying note 7.

15. *Globe* at 498 (January 30, 1866).

16. *Id.*

17. *Id.* at 498–99. The debate was unclear as to whether the Senators were discussing state citizenship or United States citizenship. It is also interesting to note that Senator Cowan seemed to concede that the native-born children of alien parents from *Europe* were citizens but insisted that those of Chinese parentage were not, a distinction that Senator Trumbull rejected. Cowan's racist position was later stated even more starkly by Senator Davis, who described the American political community as "a close white corporation. You may bring all of Europe, but none of Asia and none of Africa into our partnership." *Id.* at 529 (January 31, 1866).

18. 169 U.S. 649 (1898).

19. 16 Stat. 740 (concluded July 28, 1868).

20. Naturalization Act of 1829, 4 Stat. 310 (1829), amended in 1870.

21. 169 U.S. at 731–32 (Fuller, C.J. dissenting).

22. *Supra* notes 7–10, 13–18 and accompanying text.

23. In response to Senator Cowan's alarms about "a flood of immigrants of the Mongol race" who could "pour in their millions upon our Pacific coast in a very short time," *Globe* at 2891 (May 30, 1866), Senator John Conness of California assured Cowan "that this portion of our population, namely the children of Mongolian parentage, born in California, is very small indeed, and never promises to be large, notwithstanding our near neighborhood to the Celestial land." The Chinese, Conness continued, all returned to China sooner or later, and "do not bring their females to our country but in very limited numbers, and rarely ever [*sic*] in connection with families; so that their progeny in California is very small indeed." After twitting Cowan by asking "how many Gypsies the census shows to be within the State of Pennsylvania," Conness summarized the clause's effect: "here is a simple declaration that a score or a few score of human beings born in the United States shall be regarded as citizens of the United States, . . . "*id.* at 2892). It is also of interest in this regard that the Burlingame Treaty, *supra* note 19, which regulated Chinese immigration to the

United States but denied Chinese the right to become naturalized citizens here (and vice versa), was concluded on the very day, July 28, 1868, that the Fourteenth Amendment was ratified.

24. Senator Doolittle, for example, stated that "it seems to me very clear that there is a large mass of the Indian population who are clearly subject to the jurisdiction of the United States" (*id.* 2892).

25. This expectation of a *de minimis* effect also explains why the Citizenship Clause debate did not dwell on the exception for the native-born children of foreign diplomats serving in the United States (text accompanying *infra* note 46). Thus, Senator Benjamin Wade said of such children: "it could hardly be applicable to more than two or three or four persons; and it would be best not to alter the law for that case. I will let it come under that well-known maxim of the law, *de minimis lex non curat*." *Id.* at 2769 (May 23, 1866).

26. *Id.* at 572 (February 1, 1866).

27. *Supra* at chap. 2 notes 61–67 and accompanying text. For a recent review of the evolution of the special status of Indians in American law, including the questions of jurisdiction and citizenship, see Newton, "Federal Power over Indians: Its Sources, Scope, and Limitations," 132 *U. Pa. L. Rev.* 195 (1984), especially 216–26.

28. E.g., *Globe* 2890–93, 2894.

29. Art. I, Sec. 2.

30. *Globe* at 572 (February 1, 1866).

31. *Id.* at 2890 (May 30, 1866).

32. *Id.* at 2892–93.

33. *Globe* at 2893.

34. *Supra* at chap. 2, notes 63–67 and accompanying text.

35. *Globe* at 2893 (May 30, 1866). Senator Johnson supported Senator Doolittle's amendment to section 1. *Id.* at 2893–94.

36. *Id.* at 2895.

37. E.g., *id.* at 2897. This apportionment provision would supersede Article I, Section 2 of the original Constitution.

38. *Globe* at 2897.

39. *Supra* at notes 26–37 and accompanying text.

40. *Supra* chap. 2 at notes 68–67 and accompanying text.

41. 112 U.S. 94 (1884).

42. *Id.* at 102.

43. *Id.* The debates on the citizenship provision of the 1866 act had emphasized what the text itself seemed to imply—that this relationship was to be evaluated at the time of birth. See, e.g., *Globe*

at 506 (January 20, 1866) (Colloquy between Senators Johnson, Trumbull, and Henry Lane); *id*. at 526 (January 31, 1866) (remarks of Senator Johnson).

44. 112 U.S. at 103.

45. *Id*. at 103, 106–07.

46. Even Coke, perhaps the chief expositor of the ascriptive view (*supra* chap. 1 at notes 5, 16, and accompanying text) excluded the native-born children of foreign diplomats from birthright subjectship. See discussion in the *Ark* case, *supra*, 169 U.S. at 655–56.

The congressional debates also failed to mention three other categories of individuals who, although born in the United States, have never been deemed to be "subject to the jurisdiction thereof" and have therefore been denied birthright citizenship. The first category, consisting of children born on foreign public vessels located within the United States' territorial waters, can perhaps best be understood as an extension or variant of the diplomatic family exception, in which a kind of extraterritorial enclave of foreign jurisdiction has been recognized. (*id*.) The second consists of children born here of alien enemies in hostile occupation of United States territory. (See discussion at *id*.) This probably reflects the affront to, if not the negation of, a nation's sovereignty that birthright citizenship for such individuals would cause. The third category consists of children born in the insular territories of the United States. For example, the island of Puerto Rico was ceded to the United States by Spain in 1899. Persons born in Puerto Rico from the date of cession to January 13, 1941, did not, however, acquire citizenship at birth. Only with the Nationality Act of 1940 did persons born there after January 13, 1941, and subject to the jurisdiction of the United States, become United States citizens. These exceptions, like the one for diplomatic families, were recognized elements of the ascriptive conception of citizenship but can also be rationalized under the consensual view.

47. The Supreme Court recently seemed to endorse a different view. See discussion *infra* chap. 4 at notes 37–42 and accompanying text.

48. *Supra* note 33.

49. *Supra* chap. 2 at notes 7–9, 11–14 and accompanying text.

50. *Supra* chap. 2 at note 58 and accompanying text.

51. See, e.g., *Trop v. Dulles*, 356 U.S. 86 (1958); *Schneider v. Rusk*, 377 U.S. 163 (1964); *Afroyim v. Rusk*, 387 U.S. 253 (1967); and generally Gray, *supra* chap. 2, note 59.

52. See Tsiang, *supra*, chap. 2, note 35.

53. 8 U.S.C. 1481, 1483.

54. For the United States, see 8 U.S.C. 1481, sec. 6 (Attorney General must approve renunciation of nationality as not contrary to the interests of national defense during time of war.)

55. See, e.g., M. Walzer, *Obligations*, 99–119 (1970).

Chapter 4

1. The classic analysis of survivals in the law is Holmes, "Law in Science and Science in Law," 12 *Harv. L. Rev.* 443 (1899). An excellent elucidation and criticism of Holmes's analysis can be found in Elliott, "Holmes and Evolution: Legal Process as Artificial Intelligence," 13 *J. of Leg. Studies* 113, 129–39 (1984).

2. *Supra* chap. 2, note 1.

3. The Alien Act of 1798, 1 Stat. 570 (1798), had authorized the president to expel from the United States any alien that he deemed dangerous, but the law was severely criticized and expired in 1800. Occasional state efforts to restrict immigration during the first half of the nineteenth century were invalidated by the Supreme Court as intrusions on the federal power to regulate foreign commerce. E.g., *The Passenger Cases*, 48 U.S. 283 (1849); *Chy Lung v. Freeman*, 92 U.S. 275 (1875). In 1875, the first federal exclusion legislation was adopted; it barred convicts and prostitutes. 18 Stat. 477 (1875).

4. This strategy included easily satisfied naturalization requirements and vigorous solicitation of immigration from Europe. For a summary discussion of these policies during the colonial and early American periods, see "Immigration and Naturalization Policies in the Colonial Period and the Founding of the Republic," 2 *F.I.L.R.* Part 2, December 17, 1984.

5. M. Rischin, ed., *Immigration and the American Tradition*, 43–44 (1976).

6. 22 Stat. 214 (1882); 26 Stat. 1084 (1891); 32 Stat. 1213 (1903).

7. Exclusion of Japanese laborers was based on the proviso of Section 1 of the Immigration Act of 1907 (34 Stat. 898). This exclusion was reinforced by an understanding with the Japanese government that it would continue to discourage the migration of its subjects to the United States.

8. Racial restrictions on naturalization appeared in the very first Naturalization Act, adopted in 1790. 1 Stat. 103 (1790). They were

upheld almost a century and a half later in *Ozawa v. United States*, 260 U.S. 178 (1922).

9. 43 Stat. 153 (1924).

10. 79 Stat. 911 (1965).

11. The Census Bureau estimates that more than 2 million illegal aliens were actually counted in the 1980 Census. This number constituted an estimated 55–60 percent of the total living in the United States. For a recent discussion of the illegal immigration data, see Briggs, *supra* Introduction, note 4 at 131–37.

12. See Schuck, *supra* chap. 1, note 77 at 41–44.

13. See, e.g., N. Glazer, ed., *A Clamor at the Gates: The New American Immigration* (1985).

14. As of March 15, 1985, that legislation had not yet been reintroduced in the 99th Congress. Congressman Lungren has introduced a bill, H.R. 1061, that combines elements of the versions of the legislation that passed the House and the Senate during the 98th Congress.

15. *See infra* at notes 62–70 and accompanying text.

16. E.g., King, "Mexican Women Cross Border So Babies Can Be U.S. Citizens," *New York Times*, November 18, 1983, A1.

17. See Heer and Jackson, "The Relative Utilization of Health and Welfare Services by Mexican Families in Los Angeles Dependent on Whether the Mother is Undocumented, A Legal Immigrant or Native-Born," Population Research Laboratory, University of Southern California, paper presented at annual meeting of American Public Health Association, November 1984, at 2. This study combined an analysis of birth certificates in Los Angeles County during a nine-month period during 1980–81 with follow-up interviews with parents where either the father or the mother reported a Mexican origin. The extrapolation from Heer and Jackson's very conservative estimates for Los Angeles County does not include estimates of children born here to undocumented parents from other countries, nor does it take account of the markedly increased illegal migration to the United States occurring since 1981.

18. Telephone conversation with Dr. David Heer, University of Southern California Population Research Laboratory, November 26, 1984.

19. Although we have found no decision squarely holding this, it apparently has been universally assumed. E.g., *I.N.S.* v. *Rios-Pineda*, 105 S.Ct. 2098, 2100 (1985); *Plyler* v. *Doe*, 457 U.S. 202, 245 (1982).

20. *Supra* at notes 3–9.

21. *Supra* chap. 3 at notes 47–49 and accompanying text.

22. *Infra* chap. 5 at note 31 and accompanying text.

23. *Supra* chap. 3 at notes 41–45 and accompanying text.

24. 112 U.S. at 122–23.

25. See discussion in M. Walzer, *Spheres of Justice* (1983) at 56–60. See also, sources cited in Schuck, *supra* chap. 1, note 77 at 3–4, n. 12.

26. See *supra* chap. 1, notes 76–77 and accompanying text.

27. See, e.g., *Plyler* v. *Doe, supra* note 19; *Ruiz* v. *Blum*, 549 F. Supp. 871 (S.D.N.Y. 1982).

28. Ley de Nacionalidad Y Naturalizacion, capitulo I, Art. I, sec. II, in C.A.E. Trujillo, ed., *Manual del Extranjero* (1974) at 195; Refugee Act of 1980, 94 Stat. 109, codified at 8 U.S.C. Sections 1158 and 1101(a) (42).

29. 8 C.F.R. Section 244 (1984).

30. 8 U.S.C. Section 1254.

31. Immigration and Naturalization Service, Operating Instruction 103.1(a)(1)(ii). For a discussion of this relief, see *Pasquini* v. *Morris*, 700 F.2d 658 (11th Cir. 1983).

32. 8 U.S.C. Section 1253(h).

33. *Infra* chap. 5 at notes 8–10 and accompanying text.

34. 8 U.S.C. Section 1184.

35. Telephone conversation with Dorothy Krahn, Senior Statistician, INS, December 20, 1984. There is some overlap between these two categories, as many nonimmigrants violate their visa restrictions, remaining here and thereby incurring illegal status.

36. A large number of students and other categories of nonimmigrants, of course, are females of child-bearing age.

37. *Plyler* v. *Doe, supra* note 19 at 211 n. 10.

38. 169 U.S. 649 (1898), discussed *supra* chap. 3 at notes 18–22 and accompanying text.

39. The parents in *Wong Kim Ark* were legal residents of the United States. It is true that the Court in that case was writing at a time when severe restrictions on Chinese immigration had long been imposed and many illegal aliens were present in the country. But the Court's opinion did not address the question of the status of the children of such aliens under the Citizenship Clause.

40. The Court's textual approach, while certainly plausible, is hardly compelling. Although the Court emphasized that both Clauses use the word *jurisdiction*, it failed to explain an equally striking fact— that the framers used different phrases to introduce that word in the

two Clauses (i.e., "subject to" the jurisdiction of the United States in the Citizenship Clause, and "within" a state's jurisdiction in the Equal Protection Clause). That difference may perhaps be explained by another difference, not mentioned by the Court, between the contexts in which the word is used in the two Clauses. In the context of American citizenship, the word *jurisdiction* possesses an international law significance that is wholly absent from the context of state citizenship. Entirely different considerations, such as the fact that illegal aliens usually have another nationality to which they often can return, and the interests in national control over who may join American society, are relevant in the former context but not in the latter. It is at least equally plausible, therefore, that the Citizenship Clause used the term *jurisdiction* in the consensualist manner of Vattel, Burlamaqui, and other public-law writers who were widely cited as authorities on international law in the nineteenth century.

41. See *supra* at notes 25–27 and accompanying text.

42. See Bouvé, *Exclusion and Expulsion of Aliens in the United States*, 425–27 (1912). Bouvé's argument nicely reveals (but does not reconcile) the clash of the competing conceptual logics. Thus, he insisted that an alien may not "continue in a position of allegiance to the sovereign against that sovereign's will" (a consensual proposition), while also insisting, without providing a reason, that illegal aliens (apparently including the parents) "until their arrest . . . [enjoy] every benefit which the law of the United States confers on persons lawfully resident here" (a radically ascriptive proposition) (*id*. at 426). Bouvé continued that to deny birthright citizenship to illegal aliens "would be to deny the fact of sovereignty itself, and the existence of a sovereign right" (*id*. at 427), a very puzzling assertion.

43. For a tendentious account of the rapid growth of the welfare state during the 1960s and 1970s, see C. Murray, *Losing Ground: American Social Policy, 1950–1980* (1984). For one critique of Murray's analysis, see Greenstein, "Losing Faith in 'Losing Ground,' " *The New Republic*, March 25, 1985, at 12.

44. See, e.g., J. Palmer and I. Sawhill, eds., *The Reagan Record: An Assessment of America's Changing Domestic Priorities* (1984), chap. 6.

45. See T. H. Marshall, *Class, Citizenship, and Social Development* (1965).

46. Even this right did not extend to all citizens, most notably women and all residents of the District of Columbia. For a discussion of female citizenship, see Smith, "One United People": Discriminatory

Citizenship Laws and the American Quest for Community, 1800–1937" (unpublished ms on file with authors).

47. Reich, "The New Property," 73 *Yale L.J.* 733 (1964).

48. *Id.* at 733.

49. Schuck, *supra* chap. 1, note 77 at 4. The term was used there to characterize a set of recent ideologically related developments in legal doctrine, not a theory of the state.

50. *Id.* at 49–53.

51. 50 U.S.C. App. Section 454 (1984).

52. In effect, the elimination of peacetime conscription, like the Civil War practice of allowing draftees to buy their way out of military service, allowed citizens to convert this duty into a market transaction; a "volunteer" (i.e., professional) military force essentially monetized individuals' obligations to defend the national community from danger. By supplanting the ideal of a citizen army with the reality of a mercenary one, terminating the draft may have helped to highlight the welfare state's more general and fundamental tranformation of government's function and symbolism. From a mythic repository and executor of the nation's political sovereignty and ideals, government has increasingly become a gigantic clerk, a workaday bureaucrat, a writer of checks.

53. Some of these decisions have concerned classifications based not upon citizenship but upon what might be called "near-citizenship" statuses, such as long-term legal residence, declarant alien, etc.

54. 403 U.S. 365 (1971).

55. Hull, *Resident Aliens and the Equal Protection Clause: The Burger Court's Retreat from Graham v. Richardson*, 47 Brooklyn L. Rev.1 (1980). Note, *A Dual Standard for State Discrimination against Aliens*, 92 *Harv. L. Rev.* 1516 (1979).

56. Compare, e.g., *Cabell* v. *Chavez-Salido*, 454 U.S. 432 (1982) (citizenship requirement for deputy probation officer upheld), and *Bernal* v. *Fainter*, 104 S. Ct. 2312 (1984) (citizenship requirement for notary public invalidated).

57. *Mathews* v. *Diaz*, 426 U.S. 67 (1976).

58. *Mow Sun Wong* v. *Campbell*, 626 F.2d 739 (9th Cir. 1981), cert. denied, 450 U.S. 959 (1981).

59. This may partly explain why the rate at which legal resident aliens become naturalized citizens has declined, especially for Mexicans.

60. The percentage of eligible voters who voted in the 1984 presidential election was 53.3. This figure is derived from "Projections of

the Population of Voting Age for States: November 1984," Current Population Estimates and Projections, Series P-25, no. 948, April 1984, table A, and *Congressional Quarterly Weekly Reports*, April 13, 1985, at 687. On average, turnouts in nonpresidential elections in recent decades have been 15.8 percent lower than in presidential elections. Information supplied by Steven J. Rosenstone, May 7, 1985.

61. Although the INS does not maintain statistics on the number of legal resident aliens living in the United States, the number is certainly in the millions; of these, 608 were either formally deported or required to depart "under docket control" in 1981, the most recent year for which the INS has published statistics (*1981 Statistical Yearbook of the Immigration and Naturalization Service*, table 47 at p. 109).

62. See Schuck, *supra* chap. 1, note 77.

63. Life expectancy for a child born in Mexico in 1982 is sixty-five years, and his expected per capita income is $2,270, for a total expected lifetime income of $147,550. For the American child, the comparable figures are seventy-five years and $13,160 in income, for a total of $987,000. (See *World Development Report, 1984* [Oxford University Press 1984] at table 1, pp. 218–19.) These data, of course, are unrefined and are intended only to suggest rough orders of magnitude. To make more precise estimates, one would want to take into account the possibilities that life expectancy may be lower if one's parents are Mexican, even if one is born and lives all of one's life in the United States, and that such an individual's lifetime earnings in the United States might also be lower than average. The authors thank Dr. Oded Stark, director of the Migration and Development Program, Harvard University, for calling these data to their attention.

64. E.g., *I.N.S.* v. *Rios-Pineda, supra* note 19.

65. 8 U.S.C. Section 1254.

66. E.g., *supra* note 64.

67. For an extreme case of delay, see *id*.

68. The parents of a United States citizen, as "immediate relatives" under 8 U.S.C. Section 1151(b), are not subject to the numerical quotas on immigrant admissions. The citizen child may therefore file a petition with the Attorney General for classification of the parents as entitled to preference status. 8 U.S.C. Section 1154.

69. *Darces* v. *Woods*, 35 Cal.3d 871, 679 P.2d 458 (1984). The case was decided under the equal protection clause of the *state* constitution.

70. *The Use of Public Services by Undocumented Aliens in Texas: A Study of State Costs and Revenues*, LBJ School of Public Affairs, Policy

Research Project Report No. 60 (1984), tables 2.12 and 2.13. Of those households not detained by the INS at the time of the survey, 54.2 percent were mixed-status households (table 2.12).

71. For a discussion of the importance of marginal analysis for the proper evaluation of legal rules, see Easterbrook, "Foreward: The Court and the Economic System," 98 *Harv. L. Rev.* 4, 12–14 (1984). Again, it is reported that many alien women do cross the border illegally in order to give birth in the United States. (See King, *supra* note 16.) It is not known, of course, how long they remain.

72. Heer and Jackson, *supra* note 17, report a conservative estimate that 18.6 percent of all births in Los Angeles County are to undocumented women (*id.* at 6–7). Most of these births take place in public hospitals. See also King, "Costs of Immigration Reform, Measured and Unknown, Drowned 1984 Bill," *New York Times*, October 17, 1984, A16, col. 1.

73. King, *id.*

74. According to Heer and Jackson, *supra* note 17, surveys in Los Angeles County indicate that the flow of AFDC, food stamp, and Medicaid benefits to mixed-status families "is potentially very large"; they also suggest that for the most part, and with the clear exception of unemployment benefits, undocumented persons in these families appear to be receiving only the benefits to which they are legally entitled—i.e., benefits for their American-born children. *Id.* at 11.

75. According to the Texas study, "it is almost certain that undocumented persons contribute more to the revenue of the State of Texas than it costs the state to provide services. The opposite is true for county and local governments. At this level of government, the estimated costs exceed the estimated revenues. . . . [T]aken together, state and local contributed revenues exceed the combined estimated cost of services" (*The Use of Public Services by Undocumented Aliens in Texas*, *supra* note 70 at 88). According to the California study, which focused on Los Angeles County, "[t]he combined state and local balance sheet reveals that the average Mexican immigrant household enumerated by the Census receives somewhat more than $2,000 in state services and transfers payments than it pays in taxes" (Muller, *The Fourth Wave: California's Newest Immigrants: A Summary*, 21 [1984]). The different results in these studies may perhaps be accounted for by differences in definitions and research methodologies, differences in the benefit and tax programs in the jurisdictions under consideration, and by other factors. Both studies note that inclusion

of federal benefit and tax programs in the analysis would probably increase the net contributions of illegal aliens (*The Use of Public Services, id.*, and Muller, *id.* at 19).

76. The sensitivity of revenue-cost analyses to assumptions about unemployment effects is well illustrated by one unpublished study by Dr. Donald Huddle which purports to show that for every hundred illegal aliens working in the United States, sixty-five American workers lose their jobs, and that this yields a cost in unemployment and related benefits of $25 billion annually (See King, "Economist Views Amnesty for Illegal Aliens as Costly," *New York Times*, January 4, 1984 at A11, col. 1.) Huddle's estimates of job displacement effects, it should be noted, greatly exceed those of other analysts. See also Testimony of Alan C. Nelson, Commission of I.N.S., before the House Subcommittee on Immigration, Refugees and International Law, March 20, 1985 at 3–4. ("More than 40 percent of all illegal aliens apprehended by investigators at employment sites were in high-paying jobs. Efforts to forestall the fraudulent receipt of entitlement benefits . . . resulted in actual savings of $114 million—mostly in the western Region. . . . The program has the potential to save $10.7 billion in Federal funds nationwide." For a very different view of those effects, see, e.g., M. Piore, *Birds of Passage* (1979).

77. See, e.g., Muller, *supra* note 75. Speculating on the prospect for the 1980s in Los Angeles County, Muller notes: "Although the proportion of the people over fifty years old among the immigrant population will remain low, the number of immigrants that age and older will at least double. As a result, the demand for services to the elderly, such as medical services and Social Security, and their cost, will also rise" (p. 28).

78. 8 U.S.C. Section 1325. A subsequent illegal entry constitutes a felony, 8 U.S.C. Sections 1325, 1326, as does the transportation or harboring of illegal aliens and the inducement of illegal entry. 8 U.S.C. Section 1324.

79. For a review of polling data on the public's ambivalent attitudes toward illegal aliens, see Harwood, "Alienation: American Attitudes toward Immigration," 6 *Public Opinion* 49, 51 (1983).

Chapter 5

1. See *supra* chap. 3, notes 47–49 and accompanying text.
2. If we are correct that birthright citizenship under such cir-

cumstances is not constitutionally required, then Congress could eliminate it by statute in the exercise of its authority to exclude and deport aliens, traditionally understood to be grounded in the notion of sovereignty. See, e.g., Note, "Constitutional Limits on the Power to Exclude Aliens," 82 *Col. L. Rev.* 957 (1982). This authority would be fortified by Congress's power under the Necessary and Proper, Naturalization and Commerce clauses of Article I, Section 8.

It is arguable but not at all certain that Congress could adopt our proposed reinterpretation of the Citizenship Clause by statute as an exercise of its power under Section 5 of the Fourteenth Amendment. The courts have indicated that such exercises are entitled to considerable deference. E.g., *Katzenbach* v. *Morgan*, 384 U.S. 641 (1966); *Oregon* v. *Mitchell*, 400 U.S. 112 (1970). In this case, the statute would not implicate any federalism concerns and could not be challenged as an effort to overrule clear judicial holdings interpreting the Constitution to apply the Citizenship Clause to the native-born children of illegal or nonimmigrant alien parents (see *supra* chap. 4 at note 39). On the other hand, such a statutory change might run afoul of the hoary principle, proclaimed by Chief Justice Marshall in *Marbury* v. *Madison*, that it is the province of the courts, not Congress, "to say what the law is." This principle might be thought to be especially salient where the statute under consideration would restrict the scope of a right, as previously defined by the courts. See *Katzenbach* v. *Morgan, supra* at 651–52, n. 10. For a discussion of Congress's Section 5 power in connection with the proposed "human life" legislation, see "Report on the Human Life Bill," Senate Judiciary Committee, Subcommittee on Separation of Powers, 97th Cong., 1st sess. (1981) at 1–2. See also, Stephen L. Carter, "The *Morgan* 'Power' and the Forced Reconsideration of Constitutional Decisions" (unpubl. MS 1985).

3. Without ever having to decide the question, courts have often assumed that the native-born children of illegal aliens are citizens at birth. See, e.g., cases cited *supra* chap. 4, note 19.

4. See *supra* chap. 2, notes 9, 11–13 and accompanying text.

5. *Id.*

6. The British Nationality Act of 1981, like the Immigration Act of 1971, confers birthright citizenship only upon individuals born in the United Kingdom of a father or mother who is a British citizen or is "settled" in the United Kingdom; Part I, Section 1(1). Neither illegal aliens nor what the United States terms "nonimmigrant" aliens are deemed to be "settled"; Section 50(2), (4), (5). See *Ayam* v. *Secretary of State*, [1973] 2 A11 E.R. 765. See also, Blake, "Citizenship, Law and

the State: The British Nationality Act of 1981," 45 *Mod. L. Rev.* 179, 184 (1982) (criticizing this policy). This policy apparently antedated the recent restrictions on acquisition of British nationality. It made its first statutory appearance in the Commonwealth Immigrants Act of 1962, Section 2 (1A), which requires that an alien be "ordinarily resident in the United Kingdom." The note to the section declares that one is not deemed to be "ordinarily resident" while subject to a time restriction on one's right to remain.

7. Under French law, a child born in France but not of French parents receives French nationality (not necessarily citizenship) only if the parents are unknown or either of the parents was also born in France. Code de la Nationalité, Article 44, cited in 2 *Encyclopédie Dalloz, Répertoire de Droit International*, 379–84 (1969). In Belgium, a child born there is not deemed a Belgian unless the parents are unknown or one of them is a Belgian. Les Codes Larcier, vol. 1 (1980 ed.) at 632–33. A similar rule apparently prevails in West Germany as well. See Weidacker, "Policy with Respect to Aliens, and Migration Research, in the Federal Republic of Germany, 1973–1983," 2 *Government and Policy* 417, (1984).

8. See *supra* chap. 4 at notes 27–33 and accompanying text. The nonretroactivity of our proposed change would also be consistent with the Universal Declaration of Human Rights, Article 15(2), which prohibits a state from depriving one "arbitrarily" of one's nationality. See P. Weiss, *Nationality and Statelessness in International Law*, 2d ed. (1979) at 117.

9. Select Commission on Immigration and Refugee Policy, U.S. Immigration Policy and the National Interest at 96 (1981).

10. During the 1920s, legal immigration as a percentage of population was just under 0.4; during the 1970s, it was just under 0.2 percent, half the earlier ratio. *Id.* at 28.

11. The recent proposal by sponsors of the Simpson-Mazzoli immigration reform legislation, to make any amnesty for currently residing illegal aliens contingent upon a showing of improved immigration enforcement, may imply that such sentiments continue to flourish. (See R. Pear, "Senate Will Get Immigration Bill," *New York Times*, April 18, 1985, A18.) Given the formidable impediments to effective enforcement, such a condition would probably delay such an amnesty indefinitely. As we have emphasized, the need to alter policies in the future does not justify harsh treatment of those who are here in part because of our past policy failures.

12. Such calls began at least as early as Justice Paterson's opinion in *Talbot* v. *Jansen*, 3 Dallas 153 (1795), and have continued despite specifying legislation passed in 1907 and amended several times since. See Gray, *supra* chap. 2, note 59 at 393–96. Current expatriation procedures, embodying the 1907 act and subsequent amendments, are codified at 8 U.S.C. Section 1481, with restrictions and exceptions at 8 U.S.C. Sections 1483, 1488, 1489.

13. 8 U.S.C. Section 1481.

14. The attorney general, the secretary of state, the Immigration and Naturalization Service, the Selective Service System, or the Social Security system, for example, might be administratively equipped to discharge this responsibility.

15. International law is so adverse to the status of statelessness that it occasionally ascribes nationality against the strictures of domestic law. Thus, such persons might be viewed by international law as United States nationals, though not as United States citizens (like American Samoans). Article 7 of the Hague Convention on Nationality of 1930, as well as Article 7 (1) (a) of the United Nations Convention on the Reduction of Statelessness, which entered into force December 13, 1975, each hold that even fully voluntary expatriation should not be deemed to effect loss of nationality until the person has acquired another nationality. McDougal, Lasswell, and Chen, *supra* chap. 1, note 73 at 878, 893–94. Some writers insist, however, that these agreements should not be taken as definitive of international law, which generally permits nations to determine what actions constitute loss of their nationality unless their procedures create burdens on other states, particularly by denying residence privileges, as our proposal would not do. See P. Weiss, *supra* note 8 at 123–24, 126.

16. See Weiss, *id.* at 126.

17. McDougal, Lasswell, and Chen, *id.* at 930.

18. As Michael Walzer points out, however, this policy is more demanding than those prevailing in international law and in America's past. Walzer, *supra* chap. 3, note 55 at 106–09.

19. 8 U.S.C. Section 1481, subsection 6. In such a case, the renunciation is subject to the approval of the attorney general.

20. See Walzer, *id.* at 117–18.

21. See *supra* chap. 3 at notes 50–51 and accompanying text. The nation can, however, revoke a naturalized citizenship obtained illegally or by fraud, 8 U.S.C. Section 1451, a power that we would not deny.

22. 8 U.S.C. Sections 1423, 1427, 1445, 1448.

23. There are two possible ways to reinterpret the Citizenship Clause requirement of birth "in the United States" so as to render it consistent with a fully consensualist, nonascriptive understanding of American citizenship. Both of these seem to us too strained to defend.

The first route is to modify the public-law writers' hypothesis that all citizens obtain a guaranteed option of citizenship for their children as a condition of their own citizenship. That hypothesis gains its force from the expectation that persons would not endanger the unity of their families by permitting their nation to deny citizenship to their children. But if the parents are voluntarily residing overseas anyway, their family unity would not be so greatly threatened by refusing citizenship to their offspring. Hence, the hypothetical social contract might be imagined to guarantee citizenship only to children of United States citizens residing within the nation. But though such an interpretation would preserve the conclusion that children born of American parents abroad are not Citizenship Clause citizens while relying solely on consensualist premises, it involves too much speculative manipulation of the hypothetical social contract to be persuasive.

Alternatively, one could argue that to be born "in the United States" means to be born within the political community of the United States, and that birth to American parents in any location constitutes such a birth; this would follow because the parents remain part of the political community regardless of their geographic location, so long as they are citizens. On this reading, then, children born to American parents overseas *would* be Citizenship Clause citizens, contrary to current doctrines (see *Rogers* v. *Bellei*, 401 U.S. 815 (1971). While this result seems to us desirable, however, it would require interpreting the Clause's geographic ("in the United States") and jurisdiction ("subject to the jurisdiction thereof") requirements as being wholly identical and therefore redundant. Hence, it seems to us unsustainable.

24. See, *Rogers* v. *Bellei, id.*

25. For a summary and analysis of the legal history, see *Rogers* v. *Bellei, id.* at 830–31. For the current law, see 8 U.S.C. Sections 1401, 1431, 1433.

26. 8 U.S.C. Section 1401, subsecs. (c), (d), (g); 8 U.S.C. Sections 1431, 1433.

27. Again, the legalization provisions of the Simpson-Mazzoli legislation, which are likely to be reintroduced in the 99th Congress (see *supra* note 11), would accomplish this, albeit with undue restrictions.

28. Lopez, "Undocumented Mexican Migration: In Search of a Just

Immigration Law and Policy," 28 *UCLA L. Rev.* 615 (1981) makes a kind of tacit consent argument for more generous treatment of Mexican aliens, although he does not address the normative questions about citizenship with which this book is primarily concerned.

29. We therefore accept a skeptical attitude toward our use of tacit consent earlier in this chapter to justify provisional citizenship for the children of citizens and legal resident aliens. There, however, we believe that the presumption of tacit consent is clearly warranted, as it rests upon non-controversial psychological assumptions and inescapable practical considerations. See *supra* at chap. 2 note 8 and accompanying text.

30. For discussions of this question, see Schuck, "Immigration Arteriosclerosis," *New York Times*, September 24, 1984 at A19, col. 1; Schuck, "Immigration Law and the Problem of Community," in Glazer, *supra* chap. 4, note 13 at 299; Schuck, *supra* chap. 1, note 77 at 76–85.

31. Congress and the State Department have sought to discourage or prevent dual citizenship, especially but not exclusively where the non-American citizenship has been acquired by the voluntary action of individuals or their parents. In *Schneider v. Rusk*, 377 U.S. 163 (1964), the Supreme Court invalidated one such attempt as an impermissible discrimination against naturalized citizens. In 1978, Congress repealed several other provisions requiring dual citizens to elect one allegiance (Pub. L. 95–432, 92 Stat. 1046). For a discussion of these problems, see, e.g., Comment, "Dual Nationality and the Problem of Expatriation," 16 *U.S.F.L. Rev.* 291 (1982).

32. See discussion in *Plyler v. Doe*, 457 U.S. 202 (1982).

33. See Cockburn, *supra* chap. 1, note 3 at 192, quoting from the 1868 report of a Royal Commission defending birthright citizenship on just this ground ("it has the effect of obliterating speedily and effectually disabilities of race . . . ").

34. The equal treatment demanded by the Equal Protection Clause permits certain classifications that distinguish between citizens and aliens, and between legal and illegal aliens. See, e.g., *Mathews v. Diaz*, 426 U.S. 67 (1976), and *Plyler v. Doe, supra* note 32.

35. Walzer, *supra* chap. 3, note 55 at 112, 116–19.

36. *Id.* at 117, 119.

37. See L. Baskir and W. Strauss, *Reconciliation after Vietnam* (1977).

38. *Supra* chap. 3 at notes 54–55 and accompanying text.

INDEX

Absolutism: and ascriptive citizenship, 19; and consensual citizenship, 22–23

Alien and Sedition Act of 1798, 133

Aliens: alien enemies, 14, 154n46; human rights of, 25, 31, 48, 87, 137; resident aliens, 25, 45, 77–79, 118, 138–39, 147–48n9. *See also* Illegal aliens; Nonimmigrant aliens

Ambassadors, children of, 14, 154n46

American Revolution, 1, 49

Amy (a woman of colour) v. *Smith*, 69

Ascriptive citizenship, 4, 39, 40–41, 42–43; philosophical and legal roots, 9–10, 12–20; and perpetual allegiance, 10, 13, 17–18, 20–21; relation to birthright citizenship, 12–15, 17–18, 84, 141–42n1; and political freedom, 20–21; advantages of, 20, 133; and dual citizenship, 21

Aristotle, 28, 29

Birthright citizenship: relation to ascriptive citizenship, 11, 13–15, 17–18, 84; relation to expatriation, 17–18, 59–61, 87–89, 122, 139; relation to consensual citizenship, 43–45,

85–86, 89; advantages of, to society, 52–53, 133–34; law of other countries, 73, 118–19, 163n6, 164n7; exceptions to, diplomatic personnel, 80, 84–85, 154n6; for native-born children of nonimmigrants, 94–95, 102–03, 118–20; incentives for illegal migration, 94–95, 104, 109–12; advantages of, to illegal alien and nonimmigrant parents, 94–95, 110–12; for native-born children of illegal aliens, 94–103, 113–15, 118–20, 130, 136–37, 139; proposal to alter, 116–40, 117–19, 166n23; for children born abroad to American citizens, 126, 166n23

Blacks, citizenship status of: in antebellum United States, 2, 42–43, 54, 66–70, 72; in *Dred Scott*, 68, 72, 137

Burlamaqui, Jean-Jacques, 42; on birthright citizenship, 43–45, 58–59, 147nn 8–9; on expatriation, 45–46

Calvin's Case, 12, 16, 21, 63–64, 144n33

Case of the Postnati. See Calvin's Case

Chen, Lung-Chu, 124

169